CORPORATE DROPOUTS

FROM EMPLOYEE
TO ENTREPRENEUR

Four Eagles Publishing

The information in this book is the author's opinion only. Readers should not rely on the general information given in this book as a substitute for professional advice. The author and publisher cannot accept responsibility for any losses, damages or adverse affects that may result from the use of information contained in this book.

Published by *www.foureaglespublishing.com*
First published in Australia in 2022

ISBN: 978-0-6454618-0-0

A catalogue record for this book is available from the National Library of Australia

Four Eagles Publishing is committed to a sustainable future for our planet, people and business. We donate 1% of all turnover to environmental and social causes.

DISCLAIMER

The publisher takes no legal responsibility for the details inside the stories of this book. The words and opinions are the writer's own, the memories they describe are their lived experience and I do not have any evidence that those stories are untrue. I've chosen to trust the authors and have not done them the disservice of fact-checking every version of events. Memoirs are stories from one person's vantage point and these experiences are unfortunately, universal and this is why we've chosen to share them in this collection.

Although the publisher and the authors have made every effort to ensure that the information in this book was correct at press time and while this publication is designed to provide accurate information in regard to the subject matter covered, the publisher and the authors assume no responsibility for errors, inaccuracies herein and hereby disclaim any liability to any part for any loss, damage, or disruption caused by errors or omissions, whether such error or omissions result from negligence, accident, or any other cause.

Some names have been changed in some stories to protect privacy.

*Thank you to the women who had the courage to share
their stories and for showing the way for others to follow.*

FOREWORD

Have you ever wanted something so bad, your intentions change because of the desire you have to get it?

Well, my entrepreneurial journey started initially for one reason, and one reason only: To never put my daughter in day care and to be the primary influence in her life.

But I had to feed the businesswoman that was burning inside me … she was HOT.

Climbing the corporate ladder was like a drug, and an addiction for success. Therefore, when I decided to make the shift to quit my job so that I could run my own business and raise a family, you can imagine the ridicule and lack of support I was facing from family, friends and even my husband Brian.

"It doesn't work that way", they said.

"If you want to raise your child and be the primary influence in her life you need to reduce your work time and be a mom. Successful corporate woman give up most of their motherly duties to be successful in their jobs. You can't have both."

"It's either one or the other," they said.

"B.S.!!!!" I said. "I'll show them."

This gave me more drive to prove I could do it than a hungry lion waking in the morning to chase the fastest gazelle in the jungle … I was HUNGRY, but to be totally transparent …

Sadly, I lost a lot of friends in the process. It hurt, but added more fuel to my fire.

The first three years, I went HARD.

In the first year I replaced my income and Brian retired from his engineering position to join me in building our company and dream life for a new family.

But something happened that I believe changed the whole course of my mission.

Deep inside I was pissed at people for not supporting or encouraging this radical change. My entrepreneurial journey turned into a search for success, accolades and awards, recognition and fame instead of feeling fulfilled that I could be home with my daughter every day and earn an income.

I found frustration and disillusionment, not realizing this search was actually keeping me from the very thing I sought … FREEDOM.

For months I seethed with envy, watching other business owners and marketers succeed while I spun my wheels. As jealousy turned to resentment, I began to see the world through murky-colored glasses, finding fault with everything these people did.

And for a while, this feeling consumed me. Eventually I had to come to grips with reality: being jaded and proving others wrong was doing me absolutely no good.

- I didn't become a better marketer.
- I didn't become a better mother or wife.
- I didn't become famous.
- I didn't make any more money.

After years of feeling this way, I decided to make a change. Rather than letting external factors dictate my success, I would focus on what I could control: My Attitude.

Tip #1: Focus on passion & your "WHY", not results.

"Skills Are Cheap, Passions Are Priceless"

At first, nothing changed. I was doing my work, the same as I ever was. But internally, I was changing. Instead of a pay check or pat on the back, passion was now my most important metric.

If I showed up to my business – for love, not accolades – then I had done my job. At least for that day, I'd succeeded. And tomorrow was another day. This released me from the pressure to perform, gave me greater artistic freedom, and made my work a lot more fun.

- If nobody but me showed up to read my blog posts, I would still write them.
- If no one watched my video I would still shoot them.
- If I never got a lead, I would still market my business.
- If I never earned a dime, I would still build my business.

Tip #2: Do your best work when nobody's watching.

Wait a second. Isn't that ironic?

Aren't you trying to get us to watch your videos, work with you or buy your book?

But there's a paradox in the pursuit of fame: those who try the hardest to earn others' attention rarely get it.

Conversely, those who scorn the limelight are often the ones dodging the paparazzi.

Of course, this isn't always the case.

But with online marketing and other artistic crafts, I've found it to be undeniably accurate. Something interesting happens when you make passion your chief pursuit: People start to notice.

The world is desperate for, even envious of, people living purposeful lives that are free from fear. We are all inspired by those brave enough to shirk the trappings of fame and do work that matters.

What happens every time you see a film or read a book about some hero who risks it all to complete a quest that matters?

You're inspired. Captivated, even.

When I began build my business for passion, at first nobody seemed to care. But I kept at it, kept doing the best work I could no matter how many (or how few) paid attention. And slowly over time, people took notice.

Why?

Because there is something attractive and SEXY about passion.

Tip #3: The less you care about your audience's affections, the more your audience will be affected by your work.

Don't do it for the money

I've talked to dozens of successful marketers, authors, and entrepreneurs about why they do what they do. And they've all told me essentially the same thing: It's not about the money.

Amazon founder, Jeff Bezos once said:

"Money was never a big motivation for me, except as a way to keep score. The real excitement is playing the game. If you're setting out to master a craft, to play your own game, maybe you hope to some day become famous or rich. But if you were to dig a little deeper, you might find that such a goal isn't what you're really in search of."

Of course, there's nothing inherently wrong with money or the acquisition of it. Nor is there anything immoral about wanting a large audience or a best-selling book. It's just that those things aren't enough to fulfil you.

Because what happens on the days when nobody shows up to watch your work, or experience your art?

Do you still continue?

Not if it's about the rewards.

Passion and creation is a process, not a product

Our work is more than what we do or make. It's the entirety of effort that goes into each step of the process. In a sense, it's what we don't see.

So when you're sweating and bleeding and loving every minute of it, remember: This is the reward.

What do you do, then, when you create something you're proud of and people don't appreciate it?

Do you quit?

Give up because your work isn't "relevant"?

Or do you push forward, remembering that history's greatest artists were often misunderstood by their contemporaries? The most memorable creations are rarely comprehended by the masses – at first.

This is what makes passion so attractive.

It exceeds our expectations and sometimes offends our sensibilities. Take heart, though. Some day, someone will get it. And they will be transformed. Until then, you must learn to love the work.

Tip #4: Respect the process, and results will come.

Isn't it ironic?

You know, the Greeks didn't write obituaries. They asked only one question after a man died: "Did he have passion?"

When we set sail in search of our life's work, this is what we must seek: PASSION

Not fame or rewards or riches, but a willingness to quietly do our work, trusting the sowing-and-reaping nature of life. Remembering that good things come in time if we do our jobs well.

So where does that leave us? Where, practically, can you go from here? Strive to do your work with gratitude and generosity because this part is not you paying your dues or delaying gratification until payday. This is the best it gets.

The grind is the reward.

And if you aren't okay with that, then quit now.

Because it's only once you've mastered this mindset that you'll have any shot at making it, at getting rich and famous.

What this meant for me was admitting that my passion was building online businesses, being with my family and branding was – something I couldn't not do. And truth be told, when I was doing it for the wrong reasons, I knew it.

Constantly anxious and uneasy, I worked with apprehension.

It felt unnatural.

Only when I surrendered to the work, did I find peace – and my audience. And maybe as you chase your passion, you'll make a similar discovery and allow passion to drive you over success.

You got this ...

♡ Rhonda

TABLE OF CONTENTS

INTRODUCTION

Let me be clear, this is not a book bad-mouthing the corporate world. Some people were made to thrive there but others weren't.

Society tells us to do more, achieve more, earn more, spend more, want more. The way to do that, we are told, is to climb the corporate ladder.

There is not a one-size-fits-all way to live a life. Our journeys are as individual as our fingerprints, yet as part of the human experience we have many experiences in common.

I chose to base this book on the theme of 'Corporate Dropouts' because of my own experience with the stress of the corporate world.

As a corporate employee I spent so much time feeling burnt-out, spread thin and depressed.

I thought I was alone. Even worse, I felt I had no other options. *This is just what you have to do to make it in life*, echoed in my head, adding to my daily dread of working in what felt like a never-ending rut.

And then one day, everything changed.

I quit my corporate job.

I sought the happiness that I knew was possible in my work.

My mentality shifted to, *It doesn't have to be this way*.

And it isn't anymore.

Five years later, I continue to work for myself.

I'm a proud corporate dropout who's aware of how my own determination and ability to say, 'I don't like the way this is, so I'm going to do something different,' has reduced my stress levels.

This book was created with four groups of people in mind:

- If you love the corporate atmosphere but are feeling unfulfilled in your current job, I hope that the stories within these pages give you the kick up the butt you need to make a change.
- If you want to quit your corporate job and start out on your own and follow your passion, I hope that the women in this book give you the courage to tell whatever is standing in your way to take a hike!
- If you have quit your job and are starting out on your own, my wish for you is that you see your own potential reflected in these pages and realize that you can totally do this.
- If you have been in business for a while and are struggling, I hope that these stories give you fresh hope and inspiration to keep going. Your dreams *are* within reach!

The women in this book are truly amazing. I have been privileged to share their journey as they reveal their truths, share their struggles and revel in their triumphs. You can learn from them, take courage from them, take inspiration from them and know that you are not alone. The sisterhood has your back!

Here's to taking back control and having the courage to design the life you want – your unique life!

Love,
Tarryn.

CEO of Four Eagles Publishing
www.foureaglespublishing.com

AMY MCNALLY

FULFILLING A DREAM

It was time to say goodbye to everything I had ever known.

In 2015, my husband, Jordan, and I moved across the country from the cornfields of Iowa to the sunshine state of Florida. This was something I had been dreaming about for years. Even though I was born and raised in Iowa, I wasn't happy living there especially during the bone-chilling winters. My intuition kept whispering to me, it's time to leave, which was something I struggled with often. Who was I to leave when all of my family was here? How would I find a job? How do you even plan a move of that magnitude? There were so many unanswered questions racing through my mind mixed in with a whole lot of fears. I didn't know when it would happen, or how, but I held the faith that someday we would make it to the sunshine state. I envisioned spending my days at the beach with my toes in the sand and feeling the warmth of the sun on my skin. With that vision in mind, I started applying for positions as a therapist in Florida. I ended up receiving a few different job offers and accepted the one I felt most aligned with. Things were starting to fall in place!

Sacrifices

In order to fund the move, we sold a lot of our belongings, including my car. We also used our savings, which included money we were supposed to use for our honeymoon in Hawaii. Turns out renting a U-Haul and taking it halfway across the country is a bigger investment than we anticipated. We took what was left and put it toward the first month's rent and security deposit of our new rental home. All of these decisions felt so official. I couldn't believe this was actually happening.

I will never forget the day we left Iowa. Our families came to help us pack and see us off. After countless hugs and photos, the time had come. I took one final look around. It was time to say goodbye. My amazing father-in-law Rob drove the 26-foot U-Haul with everything we owned and we packed our suitcases and our beloved Chihuahua, Doby, into the car. We were young and naive but one thing was for certain, we were willing to take risks in order to create a better life for ourselves. As we drove away that day, tears streamed down my face. I knew things would never be the same. Only time would tell if we had made the right decision.

Arriving in Florida

A couple of days later, we arrived at our new home in Florida. We found the rental online and, based on a few photos, we signed the lease, sight unseen. We weren't sure what to expect as we pulled into the driveway. I was holding my breath while silently hoping we hadn't been scammed. Thankfully, we had rented a legitimate house. We were excited that things had come together after months of preparation and planning. I was feeling really proud of myself as I reflected back on my life up until that point. I was happily married, had obtained my Master's degree in marriage and family therapy, moved across the country to Florida, and got a job offering mental health services to children and families. I had everything I had worked my whole life for. What could possibly go wrong?

Trouble in paradise

I quickly realized I didn't enjoy being a therapist. I was trying to rationalize these feelings by telling myself that things would get better. I was in denial. I didn't want to believe I had just spent the last seven years in college and drained our savings account only for this to be the wrong decision. I didn't have a plan B, this was it. I had poured my all into becoming a therapist and moving to Florida to create a better life. What was I supposed to do now?

When you try to forge through a path you're not meant to be on, you'll be met with a lot of challenges and resistance. I like to believe this is the universe's way of helping us stay on track. After arriving in Florida, it felt like I couldn't catch a break. It was one thing after another. I am from a small town so driving through rush hour traffic in the city had my anxiety at an all-time high. I was driving up to an hour one way to see my clients. I was providing in-home therapy, which meant I had to drive to each client's home. I would often meet with one client and then have to drive to the other side of the city to see the next client. I wasn't being paid for the time I spent driving or doing paperwork which meant my paychecks were less than desirable.

I distinctly remember one day I had driven about an hour to get to a new client's residence for our scheduled session. I arrived at a very run-down apartment complex and, even though I was uncomfortable, I proceeded to get out of my vehicle and knock on their front door. No one answered. As the minutes slowly passed, and no one answered, I decided to walk back to my vehicle and call the client. There was no answer. At this point I was ready to cry. I had just driven all that way only for them to be a no-show, which meant I wouldn't get paid. As I sat in my vehicle wondering what I was going to do, I saw the client pulling back the curtain in her house and looking right at me. She was looking to see if I had left. I felt so defeated.

I wish I could say this was an isolated incident but it became the norm. I would spend my time driving all over the city and bending over backwards to accommodate my clients' schedules. The truth is, they weren't respectful of my time and they were often late for their sessions or decided not to show at all. I was slowly breaking down. As time went on, I became riddled with fear and anxiety. Not only did we drain our savings account to move to Florida but I was also starting to pay back my student loans. While my husband's career was stable and going well, we wanted to save up to buy a home so we needed both of our incomes. It felt like the weight of the world was on my shoulders. Especially because it was my dream to move to Florida and become a therapist. I felt like I had failed everyone around me, especially my husband.

New beginnings

That day in the car when my client intentionally avoided me was a defining moment. With tears streaming down my face, I silently prayed. I didn't have the answers but I could no longer deny what I had been feeling for some time, therapy wasn't the right path for me.

Shortly after that defining moment, I discovered life coaching and saw there were women who had legitimate coaching businesses. I had an inspired idea to start a Facebook group for women who wanted to "Live the life they desire". I had no idea what I was doing in terms of building a coaching business, but I kept following the nudges. I started showing up in my group and sharing posts that mostly consisted of positive affirmations and ways to shift into a more positive mindset. My mom, Teresa was the first member to join my group and her support meant the world to me. She didn't question what I was doing or why and, despite being in a different time zone, she was always the first person to comment on my posts and give them some love. It gave me the courage to keep going.

Within three months of creating my Facebook group, I signed my very first coaching client. The month after that I signed four more clients, and the month after that, I signed two more. I was ecstatic! Coaching opened up a whole new world for me. My hourly coaching fee was similar to what I was making as a therapist except I could take the calls from my home office. This meant no more commuting to the city in rush hour traffic, no more getting stood up by clients who weren't committed, and no more hours spent doing paperwork. I felt like I had hit the jackpot. Becoming a coach saved my life.

A whole new world

As I started to gain some confidence in the online world of coaching, I started sharing about emotional freedom techniques, which is more commonly known as EFT or tapping. In case you haven't heard of it, EFT is an incredible modality that offers emotional and physical healing. It works by lightly tapping on acupressure meridians similar to acupuncture in order to release blockages within the body. One of my favorite things about this technique is that it calms the body's stress response system within minutes. As someone who suffers from anxiety, I decided to become a certified EFT practitioner and have been using it for years both personally and professionally. I was shocked to discover not many people in my online community knew of this life-changing technique. At that moment, it became my mission to share EFT with women all over the world.

I quickly became known as "The Tapping Queen", a name given to me by one of my beautiful clients, and it stuck. My clients came to me with their problems and I was able to guide them through tapping and by the time the call was over, their energy had shifted and they were feeling like a million bucks. I especially loved helping women conquer their money blocks. This became my specialty. I would help women identify their limiting thoughts, feelings, and actions around money and then I would guide them through a tapping process to release them so they could shift into a higher frequency. Shortly after our sessions, my clients were celebrating major wins around money. The energy was electric!

I started making a name for myself in the coaching world that was filled with amazing women who also wanted to help others. For the first time in my life, it felt like I had a community of supportive women around me. I was asked to give live presentations, be on podcasts, and be a part of collaborations with other female entrepreneurs. All of which I was able to do from the comfort of my home. This was a whole new world to me. I finally felt happy. I was getting paid to do work I truly loved. My coaching clients showed up promptly for their calls and I enjoyed spending my time helping them. I only wish I had discovered coaching sooner.

During one of my first live presentations I broke down crying while viewers watched. While some of it was definitely nerves, more than anything I couldn't believe I was doing it. My dreams of being a successful coach were happening. At that moment I was overwhelmed with sheer gratitude for the beautiful souls who showed up to support me that day. Even though I was convinced I had bombed the presentation – I mean who breaks down and cries in front of a live audience? However, it had quite the opposite effect. People loved my realness and I signed additional coaching clients after that presentation. Not only was I helping others, but they loved me for me. This was something I had never experienced before.

Our first home

Our lease for the rental home was coming up for renewal, which meant it was time to start looking for a new place to live. While I am grateful for all that home provided, we weren't going to extend our lease and stay there another year. The neighbors next to us had a construction business and used power tools in their backyard while they blasted loud music. I set the intention to connect with a wonderful heart-centered realtor and ended up finding her while attending a local yoga class. We purchased our first home in Clearwater, Florida. Up until then we had rented homes so this was a huge step for us. We poured literal blood, sweat and tears into that home. It was admittedly a fixer upper that was at the top of our budget but I knew the moment I walked through that it was the one. We even put our parents to work helping us with various home projects when they came to visit. My mom helped scrape off outdated wallpaper, pick out paint colors, and dig up overgrown bushes. My father-in-law let us use his truck to make trips to Home-Depot and my mother-in-law, Erika, used her impressive design skills to help us create beautiful landscaping out front. It was starting to feel like home.

I spent my time trying to balance being a wife, making our house a home, and continuing to build my coaching business while still working as a therapist. The entrepreneur life was thrilling and my goal was to replace my income as a therapist so that I could focus on coaching full time.

Women started asking me if I could help them establish their own coaching business. It felt like things were coming full circle. As a result of me listening to my intuition and pursuing coaching, I was now getting paid to teach other women how to have the same freedom and happiness in their lives. Freedom to work from home, make their own schedule, have unlimited income, and do work they loved was a dream come true for me. I was finally getting to help people in an even bigger way than I'd envisioned.

Network Marketing

In 2017, I started a Network Marketing business. Admittedly I was buying the products to use on myself and becoming a business partner allowed me to get the biggest discount. However, something happened that I couldn't have anticipated. I fell in love with the products so I started sharing them with my online community. Within months I had obtained a leadership rank, earned thousands of dollars in cash bonuses, a free trip to Vegas, and I even qualified for a Cadillac. My team quickly grew to more than one thousand people. At the time I was still working as a therapist, as well as continuing to build my coaching business. With the money I was making from Network Marketing and my coaching business I had far surpassed my income as a therapist. I went back and forth for months before I came to the decision to formally resign from my position as a family therapist so I could pursue being my own boss. While I will forever be thankful for Network Marketing entering my life when I needed it the most, coaching is where my heart belongs and what I have chosen to continue to build.

What is for you will not pass you by

It's funny how we end up where we are meant to be regardless of the twists and turns it takes to get us there. While I built up my coaching business, Jordan was doing exceptionally well and advancing in his career. Remember when we chose to forgo our honeymoon in Hawaii so that we could put that money toward moving? Four years after arriving in Florida, Jordan received a promotion to be the district manager for a government agency in Maui, Hawaii. It was time to move across the country, again.

Hawaii

We arrived in Maui on January 17th, 2020, and currently reside here. It was anything but idyllic that first year. We bounced around five times until we could secure permanent housing. In case you're unfamiliar with the housing market in Hawaii, it is crazy. Undesirable homes sell for more than a half a million and finding a decent rental is like finding a pot of gold at the end of a rainbow. Making things even more complicated, the world began to close down due to the global pandemic. A lot of people were riddled with fear, anxiety, and uncertainty, myself included. However, I was eternally grateful that I was able to continue running my coaching business and scaling it to its highest income year thus far.

Despite navigating many challenges throughout our journey, some of which included: moving multiple times, struggling financially, being far away from family, changing career paths, awful neighbors and landlords, emotional breakdowns, and countless hours working, to name a few, I am pleased to share that we are still very happily married, thriving in our careers, and are the proud owners of a million-dollar home in Maui. Our home is nestled on a 2.5-acre fruit farm that is filled with lush greenery and countless fruit trees. We love going out to harvest the fruit that is in season. Some of my personal favorites include: lemons, mangoes, avocados, and guavas. Since moving here, we have adopted more than 15 free-range chickens who get to live their best lives along with a cat named Kriya. I look around at the beautiful life we have created and I am so proud of where we are. I am thankful we kept going despite the numerous challenges that were thrown our way, most of which aren't even documented in this story. Who knows, maybe I will write a full book someday. Just know that all things are possible if you believe.

Lessons

I have so much more life to live and experience and I know in my heart we have more journeys awaiting us, but I want to share some lessons that have helped me along the way.

Be willing to get out of your comfort zone.

Looking back, every pivotal moment in my life has led me to where I am at this moment. Too often people say, "You are so lucky" or "I wish I could be my own boss." I want to lovingly tell you that you are the only person standing in your way. No one is going to make it happen for you. It won't be perfect and there will be a lot of unknowns but allow yourself the opportunity to take the first few steps and learn as you go. You've got this!

Listen to your intuition.

When you feel you're being met with frequent challenges and resistance, allow yourself to check in. One of the best things you can do for yourself is take an honest assessment in the key areas of your life – health, wealth, career, relationships, etc. – and see which areas are thriving and which areas are struggling. Looking back, it was evident that I had multiple areas that needed my attention and I am so glad I decided to do something about it.

Be open to new possibilities.

I knew I wanted to help others feel their best mentally and emotionally but I didn't realize there were different ways to go about doing that. If you're not the happiest version of you, maybe it's time to expand your horizons. Allow yourself to explore topics that interest you. Read the book, listen to the podcast, attend the conference, or invest in the program. We get valuable feedback and clarity as we move forward. If you have had a desire to help others too and would love to start your own coaching business, I would be honored to walk beside you.

Last, but certainly not least, **don't settle for less than you deserve.** This goes for all areas in life – health, wealth, career, relationships, etc.

Thank you for being here and taking the time to read my first published piece of writing. I want to leave you with this – you're here to change the world. I am in your corner and I believe in you!

Acknowledgments

I am so grateful to everyone who's been a part of my journey thus far – family, friends, clients, and mentors. I want to especially thank my husband, Jordan, for always believing in me. You've supported me at my worst, and celebrated with me at my best. You're the person who knows all facets of me and yet you continue to love me unconditionally. I wouldn't be where I am without you and your unwavering dedication to our marriage. All of me loves all of you.

ABOUT THE AUTHOR
AMY MCNALLY

Amy McNally is the founder of Leadership Coaching and Women Creating Wealth, an online community for businesswomen.

She works with high-level female entrepreneurs who are ready to make more money and enjoy life. She helps her clients achieve results by utilizing her unique S.E.E method which includes strategy, energetics, and emotional healing.

With her extensive experience in therapy, Amy specializes in helping women process and release negative emotions by guiding them through Emotional Freedom Technique, also known as tapping.

This allows women to move through past traumas and deeply rooted beliefs so that they can finally conquer money mindset blocks and create an abundance of wealth.

Amy offers online coaching which includes: private one-on-one, group programs, self-study courses, retreats, as well as valuable free resources in her online community!

She resides in Hawaii with her husband, Jordan. When she's not working you can find her on her farm picking fruit, planting flowers, or spending time with her Chihuahua, Doby.

You can connect with Amy at *www.coachamymcnally.com*

Facebook Page: *www.facebook.com/coachamymcnally*
Facebook Group: *www.facebook.com/groups/coachamymcnally*
Instagram: *www.instagram.com/coachamymcnally*
LinkedIn: *www.linkedin.com/in/amy-mcnally-256936191*

ANJANI AMRIIT

THE AWAKENING SOUL: FROM BURNOUT TO BLISS

A Baptism of Fire

My body shot bolt upright, shattering my sleep, lurching me into full consciousness. Drenched in sweat, hyperventilating, a searing pain in my chest and pins and needles down the entire left side of my body. I was having a full-blown panic attack. I knew the signs well. It was no less terrifying.

My head was screaming at me, What the hell have you done? You've seriously lost the plot. We are going to be destitute, all alone, and begging on the streets!

A sobering slap of reality at becoming a 'corporate dropout'. No prior warning. No easing into it. Just a sudden full-blown 'losing my shit' kind of moment.

The week had watched me, without the slightest attempt at intervention, quit my 16+ year corporate legal career in the world's top law firms, sell my million-dollar beach pad and book a flight to India to eat-pray-love myself on some random spiritual retreat with a woman who used to be a barrister now calling herself a Guru.

Well, they say the best time to quit fame and fortune is when you're at the top. And boy, did I go out in style!

Way to go kid, my mind retaliated.

But let me back up a bit …

15

Humble Beginnings

Daughter of a Greek Cypriot shepherd Dad, yes, a real-honest-to-God shepherd, and a half Polish half Yorkshire Mum, I was the younger of two for a long time, before being bookended between two brothers.

I was raised next to a railway station, in a family of domestic violence. Home was a tiny two-bedroom, no bathroom, terrace house in the heart of working-class Yorkshire England.

Bath time was a dunk in the twin tub washing machine when we were little, graduating to a flannel wash at the kitchen sink as we grew. The toilet was outside at the bottom of the tiny concrete yard. A bucket at the top of the stairs served as our night Portaloo.

The shame I carried inside me was unknown to me back then. It was only years later, in a country on the opposite side of the world, I would find out that not every household was raised on a daily diet of Dads beating Mums.

I stuck out like a sore thumb at my all-white middle class school. My immigrant skin was just dark enough to earn the name 'Paki(stani)'. I ate my shame into submission, was known as 'fatty', bullied daily and collected one friend whose family relocated leaving me with none. A deep sense of 'not good enough' etched itself in my psyche.

I never fitted in. Not in my own family, not at school and sure as hell not in the corporate world. My earliest memories are of staring up at the comforting blanket of night sky stars, waiting for aliens to come and take me back home on their spaceship.

Raised on Miracles

I was around seven when my brother started with headaches so bad he would vomit. Endless visits to doctors and specialists resulted in a verdict … "there is nothing wrong with your son, he is just seeking attention".

Almost a year passed before they found it. A rare form of viral cancer. By then, it was too late.

At just nine years old, my brother was subjected to barbaric treatments. Head bolted to a table with a cast over his entire face and neck, with two straws to breathe through for three hours to make his radiation mask. Months of radiotherapy followed by deadly doses of chemotherapy. He became emaciated and all his hair fell out.

"It has spread to his bones," came the verdict from the oncologist after new rounds of tests. They gave him three months to live.

My stalwart, Yorkshire born 'n' bred, Nana had been attending mass at the local church to pray for him. She'd had hushed words with the softly spoken Irish Priest, who knew of a pilgrimage place in Lourdes, France. It had healing waters that cured people.

In desperation, Nana took my dying 12 kilo brother to France to bathe in these waters. After three days, he started eating. By the end of the week he was walking, talking and smiling again.

On returning home, tests showed the terminal cancer in his bones had completely disappeared. The doctors were dumbfounded.

Nana, a revered sister in the A&E department of the local hospital, took the sick to Lourdes every year after that for the rest of her life. Fulfilling her promise to Mother Mary in return for Andrew being healed.

This was my introduction to the power of the sacred feminine. It left an irreversible imprint in my soul that would profoundly affect the trajectory of my future and the future of all those I work with today.

Climbing the Corporate Ladder

Not making the grades to become a doctor, I decided on the next best thing, law. My 'careers teacher' laughed in my face. "You can't do that, you're a woman," he sniggered.

I'll show you, I thought defiantly at him.

Hailing from a working-class immigrant family, I drove myself to become the best of the best. I worked my way up the corporate ladder as a mergers and acquisitions lawyer, making it to the top law firms in the UK and subsequently Australia, after emigrating in late 2000.

Often the only woman in a room full of men, I would typically be mistaken as the secretary. I battled daily with severe perfectionism and people-pleasing. Feeling like a fraud, I worked myself harder and longer than everyone else believing one day I'd be 'found out' and sent packing.

To win my seat at this male-dominated table, I took elocution lessons, cut my hair short, wore flat boots and trouser suits, swore a lot and went for beers with the boys most nights.

At the height of my sixteen-year legal career, I was leading trillion-dollar deals, working twenty-two-hour days and flying around the world business and first class.

It came at a cost.

From the outside looking in, I'd made it. But this success brought me misery. I had sacrificed who I was at the altar of my career.

I became an emotional wasteland. Burned out and depressed. Suffering crippling panic attacks, chronic food intolerances, I dropped 19 kilos, and was in and out of hospital almost every other week for over four years. The traumas of my childhood were catching up with me fast. The road I was on was about to run out …

The Game Changer!

Impatiently flicking through a magazine in the massage therapist's room where a recurring frozen neck had dragged me to seek relief, my eyes lazily fell on a double page spread of 'Sydney's most eligible bachelors' and did a double take on one of the finalists. I recognised this stranger.

An unannounced thought dropped itself into my head, He will be in your life.

"Anjani," called the therapist, snapping me back to reality.

Two weeks later, my naked feet are tentatively ascending a narrow flight of stairs up to a meditation hall. My boss had implied ... suggested ... warned me ... to do something about my growing performance anxiety.

A fish out of water in my corporate designer heels and tight skirt I pensively press on. Reaching the summit my eyes lock with a golden-haired angel-man. Magazine guy!

We instantly recognise each other ... but not from this lifetime. He's the meditation teacher.

Dumbstruck, bewildered and dazed, my body stumbles its way into the noisy hall and dutifully parks itself on the hardwood floor.

Loud shushing steals the room. The angelic one floats in. *Here we go* ...

As I come to my senses, all I recall is being enveloped in a golden light so bright, all consuming, and overwhelming that it renders salty drops of bliss-filled tears down my cheeks. I don't want to come back. I feel like I've taken an 'A' class drug – not that I have ever taken drugs. I took half a Berocca once and it got really messy. But I imagined it would have a similar effect.

I was in bliss for three entire days.

I'd gone deep into the portal and awakened something that would never return to its box. From then on my sixth sense was fully activated.

I was about to have access to inner worlds and psychic sight I thought existed only in the movies.

The Awakening

Crunched in a foetal position on a hospital bed, hooked up to a drip. I'm on my fourth hospital admission this month. It's winter, 2004.

It had been four years since I'd left England, my entire family, sold my house and emigrated halfway around the world. I hated my job, my nineteen-year relationship was on the rocks and I was in a really bad way physically, mentally and emotionally.

Spiritual awakenings can happen spontaneously, but mostly are triggered by a personal or global crisis such as: the end of a relationship; a job loss; losing all your money or status; a loved one's sudden death; a near-death experience; a life-threatening physical illness; a mental or emotional breakdown; a war or pandemic; or a global crisis. They force us to look outside of the normal constraints of our life to something bigger for help and direction.

This particular year had two major crisis events in store for me. They came in quick succession. The end of my nineteen-year relationship, followed by an onset of PTSD (post-traumatic stress disorder). I became plagued by traumatic memories of the repeated violence I had witnessed as a kid. I felt alone, terrified and in a constant high state of anxiety.

Unbeknown to me at the time, this would be the catalyst for a complete 360-degree turnaround in my life.

Road Less Travelled

Let's now pick up from where I began this story.

My inaugural eat-pray-love Indian retreat was like nothing I had ever experienced. I received profound blessings, initiations, soul awakenings and the activation of my sacred feminine power that unapologetically defied my well-honed rational logical mind.

I was hungry for more and, at the age of thirty-four, took a deep dive into Eastern philosophies and sacred wisdoms, returning many times to India and other powerful energy centres of the planet.

I lived in ashrams and studied with Eastern masters across the globe for over a decade, learning powerful practices that restored my physical, mental and emotional health. I had the great honour of meeting one of my idols, His Holiness the Dalai Lama, on three occasions, and the privilege of studying with an Australian Guru, a 500-year-old yogi from the Himalayas, Christian mystics in America, and ultimately my Guru, Sri Sakthi Narayani Amma, in South India.

My weight normalised, the PTSD and anxiety that had plagued me became a faint memory. I became healthier and happier, connected deeply to my soul and found my purpose.

I qualified as an Ayurvedic holistic health therapist, yoga and meditation teacher, energy healer, spiritual teacher, Vedic priestess and psychosynthesis coach. I was a million miles from a shepherd's daughter from Yorkshire. And yet, I'd never felt happier or at home in my own skin.

I did any job I could find while I re-trained, sharing a two-bedroom, damp-ridden, ground floor unit with four people and my two cats.

From the outside looking in, it seemed to my friends and family that I had taken a major step backwards. But on the inside I was awakening to my true self, and became increasingly fulfilled.

Rites of Passage

After a decade of soul searching and studying ancient traditions, and with my newly awakened sacred feminine power, I knew it was time to give back.

21

My mission began in earnest around my 40th birthday. My soul beckoned me to the outback of Australia. It didn't disappoint.

The synchronicities I experienced on this trip were unparalleled. My paths crossed with a guy who was to become my business partner. It was a 'magazine guy' type of meeting all over again.

He introduced me to a beautiful Indigenous community who instantly recognised my soul, initiated me into their mob and named me 'seer'. They shared the sacred wisdom of the Tjukurpa (Dreaming) and granted me permission to bring Western folk onto their 'sacred waters' land. My rite of passage was complete. The business of my soul was birthed.

I began mentoring women and taking mixed groups on sacred retreats that would facilitate deep healing and awaken their souls and highest purpose. My cup runneth over.

Sacred Feminine Power

The sacred feminine is much maligned and misunderstood. The patriarchy has us all convinced that it's a bunch of hysterical witches dancing around a fire.

Nothing could be further from the truth.

The sacred feminine is a force or energy that transcends all gender classifications. Within us it gives birth to qualities that bring about rapid healing, transformation, self-realisation and autonomy. We cannot be agents of positive change and evolution without it.

Sacred feminine leadership traits include: intuition, creativity, magnetism, compassion, diversity, vulnerability, and a social conscience.

My corporate career was built under my own false assumption that I had to act like a bloke to beat men at their own game and get success. It almost killed me.

22

Awakening my sacred feminine power set me up for an extraordinary life. It helped me shift from a burned-out lawyer to a blissed-out social-preneur.

Today I speak with, mentor, and facilitate women to help them:

- Overcome self-sabotaging tendencies,
- Transform the narrative that women are over emotional and weak, and
- See their sacred feminine leadership traits not as a weakness but a superpower.

A sacred feminine leader is one who has reconciled their internal inaccurate self-perceptions with authentic confidence and self-worth. This happens in three stages:

1. Overcoming our own unconscious bias, perfectionism, people-pleasing, overthinking, and victimhood
2. Fostering an internal authentic connection to our sacred feminine power
3. Using our unique perspective to become a driving force for change.

Getting Results

When we lead from our sacred feminine power, we attract the miraculous.

It helped me unlock profound courage, creativity, intuition, and an ability to 'see' my clients' highest potential and purpose.

I began to get immediate and often extraordinary results for my clients. Word spread. I got busier and busier. Clients were telling everyone about me. The phone didn't stop ringing.

Over the last decade I've had the privilege and honour of helping countless women (and some men) across the globe:

- Physically – reverse serious illness and chronic pain
- Psychologically – recover from anxiety, self-sabotage and imposter syndrome
- Emotionally – leave toxic relationships; divorce amiably; find new love
- Practically – take the necessary steps to get paid for doing what they love.

The Ultimate Guide to Becoming a Corporate Dropout

I'm not going to sugar-coat it for you. If you're a budding corporate dropout, there's no quick fix. No magic pill. But the good news is, everything you need is already within you. All you need to do is turn inwards to excavate it.

Here's the prescription:

- Connect deeply with your soul and authentic self
- Stop self-sabotaging
- Lead with your heart
- Do what you love
- Find your highest calling
- Take inspired action
- Breathe through your fears
- Go beyond your comfort zone
- Be open to the miraculous
- Enjoy the ride, there is no destination
- Do things that bring you joy
- Follow your bliss and the rest will take care of itself.

Gold Nuggets

If you know your highest purpose is to make a positive impact, here are the gold nuggets you'll need to succeed:

- Trust your inner voice
- The right time to start is now
- You don't need to wait for the perfect idea to take action
- Don't quit your well-paid job without a plan in place
- Make peace with where you are right now
- Allow miracles into your life
- Accept failure is a part of success
- Learn to let go of anger, grudges or hatred
- Get a mentor
- Know that 'you've got this'!

Play a Bigger Game

I used to believe success was an external intellectual pursuit. Now I know success is being happy with who you are.

I have a corporate head and a hippy heart. Today, I marry my legal intellect with my heart. I'm grounded and bring practical wisdom to everything I do. I avoid butterfly and lotus symbols, tie-dyed anything, and eye gazing. It's unnatural. I'm no pushover, and at the same time I am gentle and compassionate.

The type of women that work with me know they came here to play a bigger game, to create positive change, and are ready to get help in making this a reality. They also know that they deserve to be happier, be recognised for their uniqueness and have their voice heard.

Following your truth is not for the faint-hearted. For some, it's about staying in the corporate world and bringing positive change to their role. For others it's about finding the strength to leave the corporate nest and launch the business of their soul.

Becoming a corporate dropout for me was not about leaving an office job. It was my journey of self-discovery and soul-awakening. A profound vehicle for personal healing and transformation and ultimately world service.

25

If you do end up working with me, then you can bet your bottom dollar on this being true for you too.

If my story resonates with you, then chances are your soul is ready for an awakening to your feminine leadership power, greatest potential and highest purpose.

Join me … if you dare …

ABOUT THE AUTHOR
ANJANI AMRIIT

Corporate lawyer, turned Eastern-influenced holistic leadership expert and women's empowerment advocate, social preneur, speaker and author, Anjani Amriit went from personal crisis to profound contribution.

After dedicating 16+ years to the cause in the top law firms in the UK and Australia, with no personal strategies to manage the high-pressure environment, she burned out.

She retreated to India to 'eat, pray, love' herself back to well-being, resurrecting the ruins of her career based on Eastern holistic practices. Over the last decade, Anjani has worked with influential founders, leaders and teams across the globe, including the likes of Apple, Adobe and Visa, fusing Eastern technologies with Western philosophies, and is regularly featured in the media.

Anjani trains burned out unhappy leaders, entrepreneurs, and executives in how to master the business of themselves to up level their potential, live their highest purpose and drive meaningful change and impact.

You can connect with Anjani at *www.anjaniamriit.com*

Youtube: *www.youtube.com/channel/UC4skyZqGeqN1ch-XUHvnleg*
Linkedin: *www.linkedin.com/in/anjani-amriit-1035543*
Instagram: *www.instagram.com/anjaniamriit*
Facebook: *www.facebook.com/anjaniamriit*

BONNIE SCHUTZ

NOT "JUST A SECRETARY" ANYMORE

I am 53 years young. My time in corporate America was long. I wish I'd dared to leave it earlier in my career. In the early '90s, a "corporate" job was any job in a physical office (not retail/grocery/the zoo (ha!)), doing traditional office work for the benefit of someone else. It was a place where you sat 8 am–5 pm five days a week and got a paycheck. These days, I assist, guide, and support others differently but recognize that my time spent in corporate was a blessing and a curse. There were highs and lows and plenty of lessons learned. I have been a career administrative (admin) professional for 31 years. Twenty-seven of those years were spent in corporate. I started as a receptionist, was a government file and records clerk, and became an administrative assistant and office manager. For 19 years, I supported VPs and C-level executives, up to helping the CEO as Executive Assistant (EA).

I didn't go to college after high school as I was not too fond of high school, and four more years of studies were not for me. I had dreams of marriage and family, which moderately came true but failed. As far as work goes, I went from my high school job in fast food into retail and customer service, then retail management. These are satisfying careers for some but not for me.

I lucked upon my first administrative role as a receptionist with the franchise office of the fast-food chain I worked for in high school. I fondly remembered playing "secretary" when I was a child. Maybe it was an early foreshadowing of my corporate career. I enjoyed that first admin job, but there was one thing that happened that I'll never forget. It makes me laugh now as a seasoned, older person.

When one of my bosses tried to find me to ask me for something, I wasn't at my desk. I was chitchatting with coworkers. When he found me, he exclaimed, "Do I have to staple your ass to the chair to get you to stay there?" Ha! This example is the first of many things that stuck out to me in my corporate life. Tales of fear and intimidation from bosses, and of feeling inadequate or under-appreciated. Stories of giving and giving and never getting anything in return.

After a brief hiatus overseas with my first husband, who was in the military, and a bit more time back in retail jobs, I returned to the US and entered corporate again. At my sister's insistence, I found myself in a contract job with the government. My official title was Files and Records Clerk. I was a single mother then and needed benefits. It didn't pay well, but I made do, and there was the potential I could be hired full-time. A few months into this tedious job filing all day, I panicked because I had not been offered full-time employment. I decided to look for a permanent role.

After a short job hunt following my government gig, I became an administrative assistant at a non-profit (through a staffing agency). I learned much about my profession and what it was like to work in corporate. Firstly, I supported the Office Manager and team. I was promoted to Office Manager, then EA to the Executive Director (ED) – a quirky guy. He did some bizarre things. Once, he was on a very late conference call and confessed to urinating in his office trash can, so he didn't have to leave in the middle of his call. Another time, when he was upset over a call, I heard him shout expletives and chuck his desktop phone across the room. Crazy!

I experienced my first bout of sexual harassment here when a doctor on the board of directors began flirting with me. He sent unwanted gifts and performed gestures that made me uncomfortable. As a young woman and single mother, I was scared. It has been a long time since then, and I don't remember every detail from the events at this job, but the impact they had on me and how I felt after is what I remember most. The long-term side effects were a hesitancy to be my friendly self and, at times, still give me an inferiority complex. I played meek and was often stepped upon.

After four years of surviving the non-profit, working my ass off for low pay, I stumbled upon an organization for administrative professionals. I joined them to learn more about my career path, expand my skills, and view their admin salary guide. The guide enlightened me. For the number of years I'd been in my profession, I made far less than people in other industries. Thus, I quit that job and went looking for a higher paid one. Job hunting during my career in corporate became commonplace – one of the many disappointing drawbacks of my chosen admin career.

Using a staffing agency for jobs was the only way that seemed to work at that time. The agencies had an "in" with the companies and often were the only way employers chose to hire. They could "try before they buy", so I get that. I became an employee of the staffing agency and sub-contracted with the company(ies). I found a fantastic job in a branch office of an engineering firm based out of California next. After securing my place and being brought on as a full-time employee (bought out from the staffing agency), their headquarters office closed my branch. I was on the street again. For me, the "street" meant it was back to the staffing agency for more skills testing and temp-to-hire placements. Luckily, the next was a massive leap for me. A corporate career turning point at a technology company. They hired me to assist a director, eventually supporting the VP of Sales. I was moving on up! I learned a lot there and grew to LOVE doing admin work even more. But … they didn't keep me. It wasn't anything I did. Instead, it was the industry and the economy. They laid off all their contractors after I'd been there for only six months.

As a single mother, losing another job was debilitating. I was young and resilient, but the corporate world negatively affected me. After these few stints through staffing agencies, I vowed to find the next job myself, and I did. It felt like it took me forever, but my spirits were lifted when I got a job for another technology company, assisting a VP. This job was my favorite job ever. I experienced some of the most incredible highs in this role, and I'll be forever grateful for that. It gave me opportunities, lifelong friendships, respect from my supervisor, camaraderie, and a "family". While there, the economic bust of tech/telecom happened. I survived five layoffs. But the toll of being privy to the pre-layoff lists affected me a lot (I realized this much later). After the fifth layoff, my boss, who seemingly was also adversely affected by his role in all the reductions-in-force, let himself go. I was "promoted" to assist a higher C-level executive. Shortly after starting with him, he assigned me a project. I was to create an organizational chart post layoff. We went over it together, and I was positioned next to him on the chart. Within days the hammer dropped. Guess what? My boss called me into his office to let me know I would "be affected" this sixth round and was let go.

I did not have the same relationship with boss number two that I had with my former boss. This guy had the gall to tell me I was a "luxury" employee. I was not revenue-generating. I was "just a secretary". I will never forget the gut-punch of being called luxury. I knew my worth. I was dedicated beyond expectation to this company and a significant contributor to its prior growth. I made it so my executive had time to generate revenue, got to meetings on time and traveled places without a hitch. I was his "right arm" and enabled him to be "present". There was no doubt to me that he recognized my contributions. I miss working with him but love that we've stayed in touch. It's been 16 years, and I have never really had a boss I liked more than him.

I was out in the job-hunting world another six times before I took a deep look inward to decide whether I wanted to keep this crap up until retirement. Was it really what I wanted? Administration was all I knew and felt comfortable with, but the wheels began turning in the back of my mind. What other options might I have for the future?

Two more jobs and a failing home-building market affected my next gigs. The layoffs blindsided me because I had felt valued and loved again. Both made me feel like my positions were "fluff", and they did not need me to sustain the business. After this, the following two positions were short-lived and not good fits. Admittedly they were roles taken out of desperation.

In the 2008–2009 timeframe, after the great economic recession in the US, I spent 18 months unemployed. After being with his employer for 25 years, my current husband was also furloughed. Together, we job-hunted for 10 of those 18 months. Unbelievable how this corporate world put us both out at the same time. We were in the same predicament and unable to live like we were accustomed to when both were working.

When I finally found my next corporate administrative job, I was elated. The commute was very short, and I was there just shy of five years before quitting. It was another roller coaster. It started great! I loved the husband and wife I worked for as the EA to the CEO. I officially reported to his wife, the CFO. After many years in lower admin roles as a clerk, receptionist, and administrative assistant, I'd finally begun to climb the corporate ladder. I was assisting the highest-level people in the company. It felt so good. But like Murphy's Law suggests, something terrible will undoubtedly happen when things are going too well.

It started with a corporate merger. Us little guys were bought by a giant conglomerate. My title was downgraded, my CFO "retired" and, though I was the Sr. EA to the CEO, I started reporting to a lower, mid-level executive. First one exec, and then another … they couldn't figure out where I belonged/who wanted me. My CEO now reported to the CEO of the larger company and was no longer top dog. He had to prove he was worthy and so had no time to manage an assistant.

Shortly after the shuffle from one manager to the next, it was time for my yearly evaluation. Every evaluation I'd had in my career up to this point was stellar. Not perfect (no one's perfect), but always more good things than bad. This time, not the case. The two execs decided to "share" me when it was time to give my review. Neither of these two had managed me for more than a couple of months during the evaluation period. They'd always been friendly to me and appeared to like me a lot. I'd never experienced any verbal reprimands or dissatisfaction with my work. Then, BAM! I received the lowest marks I'd ever gotten in every category during my review, and they put me on a performance improvement plan (PIP). The PIP was a massive punch in the gut and to my pride! I was given 90 days to improve my performance, and at the end of those 90 days, they'd either extend my PIP for another 90, let me go, or cancel it and move on.

I considered these two execs my friends, but I was mistaken. They claimed the complaints came from the CEO, and they were merely the messengers. But, if that was the case, why didn't they stand up for me or advocate for me? Why did they not forewarn me of what was coming so I could fix whatever I had done, or was doing, wrong? I was taken aback and completely shocked. I cried during my review. (That was a first.) I'd loved this job until this day. From there, it went downhill. I was a victim of corporate politics. These two middle-management execs also (like the CEO) had to prove themselves. I feel they had to find a way to make me quit by agitating me just enough so that they wouldn't be seen as the bad guys.

I struggled through the first 90 days and was micromanaged regularly. I could no longer be the happy-go-lucky me. It changed me. When it came time for that follow-up meeting at the end of the PIP, they told me I did not cut the mustard and would extend my PIP another 90 days. Another miserable 90 days? I couldn't see that happening and went home a complete basket case that day. I couldn't stop crying. I liked people to like me, and I felt unliked. I couldn't shake the feeling of inadequacy. I talked to my husband, and he told me to quit. I was ready to march back in there the next day and give my two weeks' notice. But the hubs told me to forget about that. I didn't owe them anything after how I was treated. I knew it would break me if I didn't make a quick clean break, so that's what I did.

I went to the office that night, still crying my eyes out. I left a letter of resignation on my boss's desk, along with office keys, company credit card, and four and a half years of blood, sweat, and tears. I took a stroll around the office to look at all the places I'd left my mark. Then through teary eyes, I left and never looked back. Damned if I was going to take that treatment anymore. I was NOT a bad employee. I'd gone above and beyond, I loved my job, and it showed (before that darn PIP)! That job did me in. My confidence level was low, but within a few months, I found what would be my last corporate job. It matched that of a "dream" job for an EA in my head. I was going to assist the company's CEO and manage the office. I went back to a long commute but thought it was worth it. Never in a million years did I think I could find somewhere where I would feel like I did at the last place. Respected, loved and valued. Here at this job, I found it. I was also brought on to project manage and orchestrate an office move, which was right up my alley!

As my love for the company and my colleagues grew, I got to around the four-year mark when that old Murphy's Law thing poked its ugly nose in my business again. Maybe they should call it "Corporate Law" instead? At least that's what it was for me – too good to last. I made fabulous friends out of coworkers, had an amazingly trusted relationship with my CEO and his family, and felt great! I thought it would be the job I'd retire from one day. But …

There was a new person who came to work for us. We'll call her Julie. Don't get me wrong. I'm a people person, and I strive to be kind, courteous, and friendly with everyone, even if something feels off, or if I sense they don't like me for some reason. If anything, I'm a good actress. I do not like confrontation one bit. But, when it came to Julie, shortly after she started, I began to feel her pushing the boundaries of her role and a sense of competition brewing between us. It started with a little bit of snarky emailing, where I asserted my position and my role within the company. I called her out for being on social media all day when she was "working" from home. I was the eyes and ears of my CEO. It was my job. Of course, Julie didn't like that someone was watching. She quickly realized it was me, and the tension increased. She became pregnant shortly after starting at the company and I understood the hormones so went with the flow. I even set up a meeting between her, myself, and her direct supervisor to put the elephant in the room to bed diplomatically. It didn't help.

Julie began working from home 100% during her difficult pregnancy. I noticed more and more that she seemed to be taking advantage of the situation. It was infuriating. I was there, in the office, every single day – working! Not taking walks, shopping, scrolling social media. The animosity between us was palpable. I remained professional, even though I was livid on the inside when I saw what she was getting away with "at work". One day, after the baby was born, she came into the office for a meeting. We had a little room off the breakroom/kitchen that Julie went into that day to pump breast milk. She was there around noontime doing so, and I was in the kitchen with coworkers eating my lunch. One man asked, "What is Julie doing in there?" I replied, "She's just taking a nap." I thought I was protecting her from the embarrassment of pumping her breast milk behind those doors, so near to where my male coworkers and I were. By no means did I think I was in the wrong. I'm a mother, a protector, and I understand about pumping.

It turns out that Julie heard my comment and found it to be just what she needed to destroy me. A couple of days later, I was called into my executive's office and told that HR had received a complaint about me. When I read the notification from HR, it was to notify me that I was being written up for my behavior in making fun of a breastfeeding mother (something of that nature), and I was to sign the letter in acknowledgment.

Signing the letter admitted I had done something wrong, and I hadn't! I told my boss that I would not sign it. I explained my version of what had happened and that I'd done nothing wrong. He said his hands were tied since this fell under the guise of a hostile workplace and discrimination. It was a Friday, so he said he'd allow me to think about it over the weekend and sign on Monday.

Think about it I did. I thought and thought, not just about this incident. I thought about all the things in my corporate experience that had happened to me over the years. Several left significant mental scars. At 48 I was no longer a spring chicken. I'd been in the muck of corporate mergers, acquisitions, rollercoasters, unwarranted accusations, layoffs, and uncertainty for way too long. So, I concluded that it was MY time. Time to cut the cord and let corporate life go. It was time to turn my side hustle as an administrative recruiter into a business of my own and become a CORPORATE DROPOUT. My husband fully supported me, and I was fortunate enough to get that same support from my boss when I returned on Monday. And rather than sign that paper, I put in my resignation so I could start my own company.

For years I'd felt like I was at the top of the ladder of my profession but wanted more. The previously mentioned side hustle I had was as an admin recruiter. I was ready to take it to the next level and make it a business. The recent incident at work was the final straw that broke the camel's back. It got me out there to do my own thing, on my terms. I no longer would have to deal with corporate drama and uncertainties.

Flash forward to today. I am now the successful CEO and founder of Tandem Resource Solutions, a six-figure company. I am an administrative recruiter for direct-hire admin positions. I manage a team of 30+ virtual assistants across the US, providing administrative services to entrepreneurs, small business owners, busy executive assistants, and corporate executives. I have time to participate on industry advisory boards and have found a new passion for writing. I enjoy being creative, establishing partnerships, and collaborating with others on passion projects. None of this would have been possible without the incident with Julie. It was the kick in the butt I needed to pursue my happiness and gain mental peace. I, ladies and gentlemen, am no longer "just a secretary"! I'm fulfilled and loving it and will never go back! I'm my own boss and am passionate and respected.

ABOUT THE AUTHOR
BONNIE SCHUTZ

Bonnie Schutz is CEO of Tandem Resource Solutions (TRS), based in Colorado. After a 27-year career as an administrative professional, she dropped out of corporate to be happier, more fulfilled, and enjoy her second act.

TRS helps entrepreneurs, small business owners, and corporate executives by providing virtual assistance and recruiting direct-hire admins. Other services include: resume writing, LinkedIn profiles, EA/VEA mentorship, and consulting.

Bonnie's superpower is in creating meaningful and effective relationships between executives and their assistants. She has a passion for supporting single mothers, stay-at-home moms, military wives, and women who have been aged out of corporate roles.

She is an Amazon Best-Selling Co-Author of Phoenix Rising. She lives in Colorado with her hubby and is an empty nester. When she isn't busy matchmaking, doing advisory board work, or advocating for the admin profession, she travels to tropical islands or visits her daughters.

You can reach Bonnie at *bonnie@tandemresourcesolutions.com*

Facebook: *www.facebook.com/TandemResourceSolns*
Instagram: *www.instagram.com/tandemresource*
Linkedin: *www.linkedin.com/company/tandem-resource-solutions*

CHRISTIE MORAN

WE ARE NOT HERE TO GET TO A HAPPY EVER AFTER, AND THEN DIE

I Had Arrived

I was successful. I had achieved the job that I'd been working towards for the previous eight years. It was now mine.

I bought our dream property, 25 acres of beauty, right on the river. We planned to build our forever home. I had the man I loved, three amazing kids, two dogs and two cats. What more could a girl want? Everything was falling into place exactly as I wanted it to.

So, why was I feeling so uneasy? Why was I feeling so unfulfilled and so unhappy?

It just didn't make sense.

I had spent the last 20 years achieving all that I had decided I needed to be happy and fulfilled, and to have a life that I loved. I'd achieved these things, so why wasn't I happy?

Where was the life that I loved, the life that I had been working so hard to create? I was at a crossroads, and I felt so guilty for not being happy, for wanting something more. Guilty because I had so much more than many others. And yet, I wasn't happy.

Little did I know at the time that this feeling was to open up a whole new world for me. I was about to embark on the second great journey of self-discovery in my lifetime.

Each day I forced myself to go to work and put a smile on my face. I was feeling more frustrated and less fulfilled every day. I could feel myself slipping away, disappearing inside myself. Lost, stuck inside my own life. I could feel myself becoming a shadow of who I once was. The passion and drive for life had gone. Something had to change.

As a mum, I had always needed to go to work, to receive external stimulation from the world outside my kids, for my own mental health. I loved being a mum, but I was not cut out to be a full-time mum. I needed to use my brain, grow myself, and to experience different things. So for me, working was something I simply had to do.

Where It All Began

Being independent has always been important to me. I had left home at 16, was pregnant at 17 and became a single mum at 18. I got married for the wrong reasons when I was 24. I spent five years beating myself up about not being a good wife/mum/person, because I wanted to end my marriage. I had a plan; get a job I loved and that paid me a lot of money then become a property developer, so that I could leave my job and live the life I loved. I wanted freedom to do what I loved when I wanted to do it. I wanted to live a fulfilled, passionate life and also have the finances to provide a happy life for my kids.

After leaving my marriage in 2006, I was once again a single mum. I needed to decide what was right for my family and for me. I knew I needed to work, but I also knew I had to be doing something that paid well and that I was passionate about. Since becoming a mum, I had used my work as a kind of vacation from life. Somewhere I could go and forget about home, kids, relationships and just be me.

I secured a great job as a Branch Manager at one of the largest building societies in Australia. I worked hard to progress and successfully achieved my goal to become a Regional Manager. This was a great organisation, with great people and I got to support and develop others. During my 13 years with the organisation I had grown and changed. For the first 10 years I had loved my job but my role had changed over the years, and I was beginning to dread going to work every day.

By this time I had renovated four houses and built another and I was feeling the pull back to property again. I decided it was time. I wanted the freedom that I believed I could only get by being a property developer. I bought a site on which I was going to do a townhouse development. It seemed like a great idea at the time. I wanted to leave my corporate job and I thought this was my ticket out. As I started to progress with this, the fear threatened to stop me on a number of occasions. I had not done anything like that before. All the doubt and fear were paralysing at times, "How do I even do this? This is a lot of money. I'm out of my depth. I have no experience. What if I totally stuff it up? What if I lose everything?" After all, I had not built five townhouses before. I was way out of my depth.

I began a Life Coaching certification course to help me overcome my fear. It was interesting that on the first day I realised that if I became a property developer, I would no longer get to be a coach. Coaching is the thing that I had loved throughout my entire career. I realised that property was a means to an end (supposed freedom), not the means to a passionate life. This was a massive realisation for me. All of my life I had been chasing this dream of being a property developer when, in actual fact, it was the coaching that had brought me so much happiness all along. And I was on the brink of giving it all up.

At A Crossroads

I was having lunch with my 24-year-old son. We were talking about his upcoming wedding when he mentioned that he and his fiancée were planning to have a baby soon after the wedding. I had always wanted to be a hands-on grandma. My quest for more freedom had just become more urgent. I decided the thing to do would be to quit my job and start my own coaching business. One part of me thought, "What a great idea!" but the other part of me said, "You've just bought 25 acres, and in the midst of building our dream home. What are you thinking? You're crazy."

To build the dream home, I needed to get another mortgage. So, if I went down that path, I was stuck in that corporate job to pay the mortgage. It wouldn't just be telling the family, "Hey, I'm quitting my nice secure job, that pays me really well. We're also not building the new house." I felt so guilty! I was going back on my promise, because "I wanted to be happy." My daughter was 16 at the time and she said to me, "You can't just quit your job. We have a mortgage to pay." In that moment I was proud of her for being so responsible, but it also broke my heart. I realised that I had been prioritising money, property and security over my dreams. That was what I had taught her as well.

I wanted my kids to live their dreams. I realised that if I couldn't take a risk to live my dreams, then how could I teach my kids to live theirs? The only way I could teach them was to show them it is possible.

When I started to tell the rest of the family that I was going to quit my job and start a business, they were apprehensive. Even though their concerns came from the right place, it did have an impact. It raised doubts about whether I could do this, if this was the right thing to do, and if I could really make this work. But honestly, what was the alternative? To stay in a job that I was no longer happy in for another 20 years? As far as I was concerned that was not an option. Trust me, there was a lot of work I needed to do to overcome these fears and doubts.

The day I resigned I spent the whole day stalking my Executive's office door, waiting for a free moment, which I didn't get until after five. It was so nerve-racking; it was a really tough conversation to have. I was giving so much up. Of course he asked, "What are you going to be doing?" That was the hardest part. I had no job to go to, just an idea for a new business, one that I would be happy in. A lot of people said I was crazy, that I should have started with a side hustle. I couldn't do both at once. My job was too demanding, it was long hours and emotionally draining. If I had tried to start a business and maintain that job, neither of them would have been done well. And so I made the decision to quit my job and jump in with both feet.

My Journey of Self-Discovery

The journey of self-discovery had begun. One of the biggest fears I needed to overcome was the fear of losing the people I loved. Underneath it all I thought that "If I failed, I would lose everything. My partner and my kids would hate me. They would all leave and they would never forgive me, and I would be alone and unhappy forever." Up to this point I was trying to do everything and be everything in order to make everybody else happy so that maybe I could be happy too. That was what was driving me – I really wanted to be happy.

When I realised that I needed to put my needs first, there was so much guilt. Guilt about leaving a good job; disappointing the people around me that believed this was the perfect job; for leaving the team that were reporting to me; for not building the new house that I had promised my daughter; for the extra pressure that I put on my partner. So guilty for putting me first, instead of everybody else. I had to keep reminding myself, "If I'm not putting myself first, then that's all I'm teaching my kids. If I'm not putting myself first, I can't be the best version of me and so my kids are missing out, the world is missing out." So many of us are raised by generations of mothers who put everyone else first. They have been teaching the next generation of girls that this is how it is done. Well, no more! I wanted my daughter to put herself first, to know she is worthy of having her needs met and living a life she loves. And that, in order to be the greatest contribution to others and to the world, putting herself first is absolutely necessary.

There was a lot of resistance, fear and guilt to let go of to create this business. As I did that, then I knew it didn't matter if I stuffed it up and lost everything. I had done the work to be really confident in the fact that my family weren't going to leave me and even if they did, I would be okay.

Unfortunately, it didn't just end there though. When we are growing and evolving and creating new things, we are constantly pushing our boundaries. The first 18 months in business felt as though I was constantly living miles outside of my comfort zone. After I started my business, I hired office space on a three-year lease. Two weeks later we had shut down for COVID. So that was fun. Before resigning I had put the town house development on the market and contracts had exchanged. The property was due to settle the following month, the tenants vacated ready for settlement. Everything was going to be okay; this was my back-up plan. But the property sale didn't go through. The purchaser could no longer get finance. I found myself with no job, no tenants to cover the mortgage, unable to begin my face-to-face coaching business and I had office space that I was paying for and couldn't use. I remember driving to my son's house one day and needed to pull over on the side of the road because I couldn't stop crying. In that moment I couldn't see a way out.

It was beginning to feel like obstacle after obstacle after obstacle. At any of those moments, I really could have thrown in the towel and asked for my job back. I would be lying if I didn't admit I considered it. I am so grateful to the friends and mentors I had met through my Life Coaching studies. Using what I had learned and tapping into the support of these people meant the tears and meltdowns never lasted long.

I kept coming back to what it was that I was trying to achieve. I wanted to live a passionate, fulfilling life. And if I went back, I would just be stuck there again. I knew I had to stay on this journey of discovery, overcoming the obstacles presented at what felt like every turn. I knew I could create something great. If I had given up, or not left my job at all, there would have been so many people that would still be struggling, still hating life, because they didn't get the opportunity to work with me. I wouldn't be setting the example for my kids that I am today. I wouldn't be writing this chapter or the chapter I had published in *Phoenix Rising* or any of the other amazing things I am doing. I love supporting people like you, who have reached a crossroads in their life or career. Empowering them to let the past go as they create the life and career they always dreamed of but maybe thought would never be possible. It's my intention to empower millions of courageous people to not just choose the path that is true for them, but to live it.

That wouldn't have been possible for me if I had given up or given in to the challenges, the fear, the doubt, the guilt, if I went back just because things were getting tough. Well then, what else would I be missing out on? What else would the world be missing out on? I am here to make a difference. I am here to live a passionate life, and to empower others to do the same.

I think it's really important for us to share our stories. I know that there are so many people out there who are feeling trapped in their life. Whether that's because they've been trying to achieve success in their job, trying to find the perfect relationship, or trying to build the perfect life and have got lost along the way. You see people striving for the next thing that will make them happy. "I just need to buy the car and then I need to buy the house, get married and I need to have 2.5 kids, and then I will be happy." But it doesn't work like that. These things don't give you that fulfilment and happiness.

We Are Not Broken

Life really started to get good when I truly accepted that I wasn't broken and that I didn't need to fix myself. I am not broken, and I never was. You are not broken, and you never were. When we accept this and focus on what we want rather than what we had, we are free to create what we want. I don't know about you, but if I'm about to dive into the big blue ocean of life, I'm going to leave my baggage on the shore. When the ocean gets rough it's hard enough to keep your head above the water. You don't need excess baggage weighing you down.

If you want to step into your purpose and wake up every day excited to get out of bed and live an inspiring life, then you need to be creating that now, in the every day, not problem-solving the past.

I want to make it clear, life is not a destination. We are not here to get to a happy ever after and then die. It is a journey. We are here to experience every day, and to love every day. We are not here for life to be shit, all the way up until we get our happy ending. We are also not here to stay living in our past trauma and drama. Life is the journey, and that journey begins with connecting with you, and loving you. I could not have overcome all that I have without first having that foundation in place. You have to be your own cheer squad and have your own back. It all starts with YOU!

I will end this chapter with a poem that came through to me from my guides during one of those challenging moments. I believe these words were not just for me, but also for me to share with you.

You Are Already Enough

It's okay my darling, you have already created it.
It's coming with great force.
It's coming; I know you can feel it.
It's been growing in size and in anticipation.

Your creation is done.
Keep following your creative spirit.
Keep following your light.
Breathe deeply, as this enhances your light.

Shine brightly so they can see you.
They are on their way.
Don't huff my dear, everything is okay.
Your creation is done. It's time to allow the magic.

Breathe. Breathe.

Notice when you breathe, you can feel it.
It is on its way.
Soon you will be able to touch it.

ABOUT THE AUTHOR
CHRISTIE MORAN

Christie Moran is an empowerment coach, a multifaceted energy healer, and a heart-centred business owner. She is an International #1 Bestselling Author. She is also the creator of transformational programs for courageous people committed to living an authentic and impactful life. Her work combines inner mindset work and energetic transformation, supported by a strategic framework designed to empower.

Christie's soul-burning passion is to facilitate courageous individuals to experience maximum impact through their deepest level transformation and to guide them to connect with their inner fire and step into what is true and fulfilling for them.

Christie lives in Australia and works with people all around the world. In her spare time she enjoys being a grandma and volunteering as a mentor to teens at risk of disengagement.

Linktree: *www.linktr.ee/christie.moran.980*
Website: *www.wholisticlifetransformations.com*
Facebook: *www.facebook.com/christie.moran.980*

Free Community Hub: www.wholisticlifetransformations.app
Facebook Page: www.facebook.com/wholisticlifetransformations
Linkedin: www.linkedin.com/in/christie-moran-creatingyourlife-business
Instagram: www.instagram.com/christie.moran.980

ELIZABETH CHRISTIES

CHASING SUCCESS

"Who looks outside, dreams, who looks inside, awakes."
Carl Jung

Introduction

I have just arrived at the Regent Chiang Mai in Thailand, the most, exotic luxurious resort I have ever stayed at in my life up until now. My husband and I are escorted to our Garden Villa room with amazing views of the rice terraces and the resort pool. The 20 acres of lush plantation has an air of exclusivity about it. The villas are all strategically positioned so it feels as if we have the whole resort to ourselves. In the background I can hear the sound of the local water buffalo and wildlife. A huge sense of accomplishment and achievement washes over me as I take in the sights and sounds of this incredible resort. At the age of 29, I have finally made it.

Celebrating and the "Call to Adventure"

Only a month prior, I had just been offered and accepted a dream job with a top Global Investment Bank. This called for a celebration and my husband and I decided to splurge on a luxury escape to reward ourselves before packing up our lives in Melbourne and relocating to Sydney.

This was my call to adventure, as I have always been a restless soul, looking for the next challenge, the next mountain to climb. Up until this point, I had already had five jobs, my longest a three-year stint before finally arriving in the world of Investment Banking. I was ambitious, highly driven, focused on getting ahead in life, always looking for and chasing the next opportunity to keep my overactive mind stimulated and for the next prize. In some ways, I envied some of my university friends who had chosen and found their dream corporate careers earlier on. They seemed more settled and satisfied whereas I always had the feeling that something was missing and I needed to look for something more.

Somehow, my competitive nature was always driving me forward to expand myself, to get out of my comfort zone and create a life of purpose and meaning and to ultimately achieve success.

"Success" as I defined it back then was climbing the corporate ladder and attaining a high status, a job title, money, wealth, and a reputation for being excellent at what I do. I was craving recognition, acknowledgment and being valued by the businesses and clients I served. I achieved this by a lot of hard work and effort, and overcoming any obstacles on the way. I also set high expectations for myself, always striving to do my best, and always looking for ways to continuously improve, learn and grow. Little did I know this single-minded focus and determination to achieve the end result, (which I thought at the time was one of my greatest strengths), was actually going to be my undoing –" The rise before the fall".

Making the move and seizing the moment

We moved to Sydney soon after returning from Thailand and settled in Cremorne Point, a lush green suburb with steep hills and winding roads right on the harbour, a welcome change from the flat, well laid-out, suburbs of Melbourne. The smell of the frangipanis, the star jasmine, the jacaranda trees and the subtropical landscape had an almost "holiday feel". It was exciting catching the ferry to Circular Quay and taking a short walk up the hill to Chifley Tower for my first day of work at the Investment Bank.

I had high expectations of what my future would hold and I was not disappointed. The staff and management were welcoming, there were lots of "meet and greets" and as I got a tour of various senior executives' offices, the board room and the trading floor, my eyes took in the expansive views of Sydney Harbour, the glistening water, the yachts and ferries and the dazzling blue sky. Sydney never fails to impress a first-time visitor as the harbour is something truly magnificent to behold. Melbourne's muddy brown Yarra River that I was accustomed to was no match for the dazzling harbour.

I quickly absorbed the energy of the trading floor. Everyone seemed to have a real sense of purpose, a drive to achieve results. I was swimming in a sea of high achievers, "A type" personalities, the best and brightest. The sales traders, proprietary traders, research analysts, and investment bankers worked hard and played hard. They were serious, they were switched on, they were direct, driven, logical. Others were charming and charismatic, they had presence, they were polished and well presented, articulate and knew how to build business relationships, how to make connections, how to pitch clients, and get deals done.

I also was impressed with the diversity of the organisation. Staff were from the UK, Ireland, India, Hong Kong, America and Canada together with the local Australian staff. However, I quickly sensed that this international melting pot was not a place for introspection. This was a place to get things done, a place of action-taking, decision-making, everything was "urgent and important". This was the big end of town – corporations, institutional investors and sophisticated investors. It was a badge of honour to be "busy" and "stressed". Everything was about achievement and the end result. This new environment should have made me nervous, anxious, maybe even slightly stressed – it was certainly enough for my inner critic to start doubting myself." Am I good enough to be here?" "Do I belong?" If I felt it, I wasn't showing it. I was here to put my head down, to learn quickly, to adapt, to grow. Somehow I had the inner belief and confidence that I would figure it all out, after all, "Failure was not an option".

After the quick internal pep talk, I was led to my office and met a legal secondee from a top tier law firm. I would be working with them to fulfil my brief of providing advice and managing regulatory and reputation risk of the Australian businesses, which included stockbroking, investment banking and proprietary trading.

Ascending the peak

I sat at my desk and familiarised myself with the policies and procedures and reviewed the organisational chart. It showed I had dotted lines to the local Australian Business Unit Heads and a hard line to my boss in Hong Kong, who was Head of Asia Pacific. This reporting structure excited me as I had always managed to attract and find roles with a high level of responsibility and autonomy. I loved making decisions, providing advice, being curious, creating something new, looking for opportunities to innovate and I had the perseverance and long-term focus to see it through.

Little did I know at the time but these qualities and characteristics were my inner "entrepreneur", the one seeking freedom, seeking flow and seeking fun. I had the inner constitution, strength and determination to overcome any obstacles and challenges that came my way as I ascended the mountain to reach the peak. Back then, I was seeking safety, security, stability, and the only way to achieve this in my mind was a well-paid corporate job.

The first few years were stimulating, challenging and fun. Every day was different and fuelled my need for variety, significance and growth. I worked hard during the week and weekends were left for exploring our new surroundings: Balmoral Beach, the Spit Bridge to Manly walk, hiking, swimming, catching the ferry to Watsons Bay, walking along the cliff tops from Bondi, Tamarama to Clovelly.

The weekends felt like a holiday as, apart from what I have already mentioned, there was always something new to do: a day trip, Paddington Markets, the South Coast, weekends up past the Hawkesbury River to Terrigal and beyond, a ski trip to Perisher and, in between all the work, some great overseas holidays to Europe. We also had lots of time to relax, read the newspapers, drink coffee, eat out at nice restaurants, take in the views, visit galleries, go to the theatre and see live concerts.

One big highlight was going sailing with some friends who were visiting from Melbourne. We sailed from the Cruising Yacht Club in

Darling Point to Middle Harbour where we moored overnight before taking turns steering the yacht back into Sydney Harbour. This water playground was exhilarating and certainly nothing I would have experienced back in Melbourne. Money was flowing, we were having an adventure and life was fun.

In just under two years since starting this new job, I was promoted to the title of "Vice President" and as soon as I had received that title I was thinking about the next promotion to "Executive Director". I had been recognised for my ability, my integrity and reputation for giving sound advice. The Stock Exchange had also recognised my work in a recent review where they rated us in the top ten percent of brokers for our regulatory processes and procedures. I was filled with a sense of pride that I had played a large part in achieving this rating. I felt aligned, on track, it spurred me on to work harder, to see what else was possible. Maybe a possible posting overseas – Hong Kong or London – some of my colleagues had even moved to New York.

This environment was intoxicating: the international travel, the conferences, flying business class, staying in five-star hotels and meeting Business Heads in Hong Kong. Briefing them gave me a sense of importance, that I was knowledgeable, and this fuelled the fire within and kept me performing to a high standard. I focused on all the external trappings of corporate success. I reassured myself I had what it took to reach the top.

Obstacles and the beginning of the fall

But slowly and steadily things changed, reaching a crisis five years in, when I started getting swallowed up by the volume of work. The projects got bigger, the hours became longer, the day-to-day demands unrelenting. The pressure was building. The weekends were no longer opportunities for adventure, rather they were times for collapsing into bed exhausted, depleted, tired to the bone. I wondered why I got headaches late on a Friday and then have to spend the entire weekend in bed. My body was trying to communicate with me, telling me to slow down, to rest, and then miraculously I would recover by Monday morning and jump out of bed only to do it all again.

My body started talking even louder – frequent migraines, skin rashes, breakouts, digestive issues, viruses. My immune system was so low that it finally led me to see a doctor who tested and confirmed I had glandular fever. Despite this diagnosis I didn't take a day off work. I ploughed ahead as there was too much to do, and not enough hours in the day to take a sick day, let alone a week or two. I had become a workaholic, addicted to the dopamine hit of getting tasks and jobs done. An internal reward for meeting the deadline or exceeding expectations on a project followed by a feeling of relief until the next dopamine hit. My life slowly and surely had turned from a dream to a nightmare. I realised I had no boundaries, I had no balance, I had lost sight of who I was. My self-care was non-existent as I was so caught up in doing, fixing, advising, forcing and controlling. I had forgotten how to be a human "being".

During this time, I maintained a calm and composed exterior but the cracks were beginning to show. I would perform all day, keeping up the veneer of competence, capability and being in control and then at night, I would get home irritated, frustrated, angry, reactive and have difficulty sleeping because I couldn't switch off, I couldn't relax. I was also venting a lot to my husband about my day. Thankfully he was a patient and good listener but this was not how an ideal relationship should be. I was using him as my dumping ground for the drama that had unfolded during my workday. I was self-centred and self-absorbed in my own world of pain. In contrast, he seemed to cope with the demands of his job better than I did, somehow able to compartmentalise events of the day and switch off when he got home. I was letting my emotions get the better of me and I had no way to process them effectively so I bottled them up for another day.

Now, instead of feeling fulfilled, happy, inspired, excited, I was slowly starting to feel like I was running on empty. I felt a void. I started to feel disconnected, no longer interested in the work, no longer motivated to achieve and wondering where the exit sign was. One particular day I was wondering whether I was on the verge of "burnout" and I boldly asked my boss, "When will I have some down time?"

Surprisingly, through this turbulent time, something remarkable happened. I got pregnant. I was not sure how it was even possible with the amount of stress pulsing through my body, but somehow this was the exit sign I had been looking for. I would continue to work hard for the next few months and then go on maternity leave. This would give me the time and space to press "pause" on the corporate world and allow me to restore and reset myself before deciding the next step.

Balance and renewal, followed by the fall.

When my son was born, life changed for the better. I felt the happiest I have ever been in my entire life. The hard edges of my personality started to soften. I got "out of my head" and "dropped into my heart" and the caring, passionate, creative, nurturing side of me emerged. I started seeing life through a new perspective, a new lens. I decided, then and there, that I was going to enjoy every moment.

By the end of 12 months of maternity leave I decided I couldn't return to a demanding corporate job and juggle motherhood at the same time so I resigned. My boss was shocked as he was not expecting this from me. When he asked me what it would take for me to stay, I said a role working two to three days a week from the Melbourne office (as while on maternity leave I had enjoyed spending some time back in Melbourne with family and old friends) Surprisingly, he said he would go away and think about it and, to my delight, he created a regional project role for me. I felt appreciated and recognised and I was quick to jump back into the corporate fold.

The next four years before the birth of my daughter were a turning point for me as I finally thought I had found the magic pill – I could have a successful career and balance it with motherhood – but this too was short lived. After another stressful time where work demands changed and I was roped into parts of my old job, my health started to suffer. During my second pregnancy I was diagnosed with pre-eclampsia. I needed to slow down or I would risk not only my own health but also my unborn baby. I decided this was the sign from the universe to "drop out" of the corporate world and, just in time to receive my last paycheque that included an end-of-year bonus, maternity leave and long service leave entitlements. This lump sum would keep me financially until I figured out my future career options.

I then made the decision to throw myself wholeheartedly into motherhood. After all, this was also a full-time job, just without the paycheque. Unfortunately, full-time motherhood was not the panacea I was looking for. I was now 39 and the second time around as an older mother, I was tired, I was depleted and I had not learnt my lesson. Instead, the loss of "a work identity" resulted in me applying my workaholic and perfectionist tendencies to motherhood. I kept myself busy but I was mentally unfulfilled. I got involved in fundraising opportunities at the kinder and helped out in the classroom as a parent helper, hoping this would fill the void. I also kept myself busy on the domestic front, cooking, cleaning and keeping up appearances that I was a competent housewife and mother but I was soon running on empty again, repeating my well-worn patterns.

A few short years later, I was diagnosed with a chronic illness, which stopped me dead in my tracks. Life came to a standstill and I now felt stripped bare. The truth was I was a burnt-out workaholic with no boundaries, no balance, no self-care, and not in touch with my true self. Now with a chronic illness, I had no choice but to look within.

The truth will set you free

The journey within was painful, uncomfortable, an emotional roller-coaster. I suffered PTSD, felt anxious, I was overthinking everything. I oscillated between procrastination, overwhelm, and perfectionism. This resulted in getting hardly anything done on a day-to-day basis. Simple tasks seemed too hard and the high-achiever identity was a thing of the past. I was a shadow of my former self, feeling hopeless, depressed, on edge, and in a constant state of hypervigilance. I was exhausted. My mind was not my friend. Hardly the picture-perfect image of a woman having it all.

I did eventually reach out and get some help. A naturopath helped me detox my body, change my diet and, for the first time in years, I felt well. I had energy and vitality again and thought I could consciously create a successful life by design rather than living according to others' expectations. I also used a psychologist and an energy healer who helped create some awareness around my rigid thinking, limiting beliefs and helped me to clear out some unprocessed emotions. Suddenly I was feeling hopeful again and I put my mind to thinking about who I wanted to become in the next chapter of my life. This time I was determined to find success from the inside out.

Over the next few years I began exploring what I truly wanted, what truly mattered to live a fulfilling life. This led me down the path to where I am today. I studied energy medicine, matrix therapies, passion and purpose coaching, masculine and feminine coaching, neuroscience and human behaviour, including Neuro-Linguistic Programming to understand how the mind works, and how to use an empowerment model of coaching to create change. I also learnt to slow down by meditating and breathing more deeply to reset my nervous system. I encourage everyone to experiment and find their own personal medicine.

In February 2021, I took the plunge and set up my own coaching business where I work one-on-one with high-achieving professionals and business owners to achieve their desired result. In particular, my mission is to help high achievers who have been chasing outer success find deeper connections and true fulfilment.

I also have plans in the not-so-distant future to facilitate "Escape the World" retreats to create a sacred space for people to "pause", slow down and contemplate what they really want, restoring and rejuvenating their soul before seeking the next adventure in their life.

Finally, after the roller-coaster journey I have been on in the corporate world, I thought I would share some of the lessons I have learnt in the hope that it helps you maintain your relationships, health and wealth and prevents you from falling into the same pitfalls and traps.

Key lessons from my journey

1. Learn to manage your inner critic and avoid self-sabotage to gain clarity and confidence so you can achieve more in less time and lead a more fulfilling life. This will also do wonders for your energy levels as you let go of what is no longer serving you.

2. Know yourself by becoming aware of your underlying motivations and values to create a life that is authentically yours and allows for your true expression.

3. Enjoy the journey and "be present now" rather than ruminating in the past or worrying about the future.

4. Learn the wisdom of your emotions as they are truly the doorway to the soul. By understanding this language you can become more emotionally resilient and respond to life more resourcefully rather than reacting, which will create more peace and acceptance in your life.

5. "Let go" of the logical mind by surrendering "the need to know everything". The mind thinks, the heart knows. By tapping into your intuition and following the subtle signs and symbols, you will be able to access your creativity, imagination and new opportunities beyond what your logical mind thought possible will unfold. This is a vital skill for anyone in life and, particularly, entrepreneurs.

6. Regularly ask yourself what your personal needs are so you are making them a priority in your daily life. Everyone has a need for security, variety, love and connection, significance, growth and contribution. Which ones are important to you at this stage of your life? Also, think about what simple things you can do to release more happiness hormones e.g. dopamine, oxytocin, serotonin and endorphins, rather than running your life in a constant state of busyness and stress.

7. Challenge what you are saying "yes" and "no" to on a daily basis so you can understand whether you are doing things out of expectation and obligation instead of respecting and honouring your own truth.

8. If you have fallen victim to workaholic or other addictive behaviour, ask yourself what are you avoiding? Are you comfortable in your own company? If not, it is time to ask more questions. What are you running away from?

9. Change and transformation is not easy but there is a process that, when followed, allows you to become a conscious creator in your life. Believe in your infinite potential and take inspired, imperfect action to achieve your desired result.

10. Learn to use your energy wisely. Look after your physical, emotional, mental and spiritual wellbeing because your health is your greatest wealth.

11. Have the courage to ask for help by leveraging the knowledge and wisdom of someone who has already achieved the balance and inner peace you are seeking.

12. All change happens by taking a series of small consistent steps and holding yourself accountable.

Today I have created more balance across all areas of my life and, as a result, I am able to maintain my health and wellbeing. I have deeper connections with my relationships, family and friends and I make time to prioritise the things I love, spending time in nature, and having adventure and fun.

And in my business, I am now living my mission, purpose and passion, helping high achievers overcome challenges and obstacles so they can lead more aligned, authentic and fulfilling lives.

I also have a much greater acceptance and appreciation for my life as it is, in all its imperfections, rather than chasing success outside myself.

Finally, and most importantly, I have learnt to slow down, pause and realise life is not a race. Stop and enjoy the journey. Life is beautiful and there is no better time than the present moment to create a life you love.

ABOUT THE AUTHOR
ELIZABETH CHRISTIES

Elizabeth Christies is a Certified Results Coach, Mentor, Author and Soul Realignment Practitioner.

After years of climbing the corporate ladder and achieving outward success, Elizabeth was no longer feeling fulfilled.

She then dedicated the next ten years of her life on a journey of personal development to reclaim her wellbeing and discover how to achieve success from the inside out.

The culmination of this work is the foundation of her coaching programs that combine mindset work, emotional release techniques together with a strategic change work framework to empower clients to consciously create the results they desire in life.

Having reached her own turning point in life, Elizabeth's passion, purpose and mission in life is to help high achievers overcome challenges and obstacles so they can lead more aligned, authentic and fulfilling lives.

Elizabeth lives in Melbourne, and currently works with clients all around Australia and is excited to support new clients worldwide . In her spare time, she enjoys walking her dogs, spending time in nature, and planning her next adventure with her family.

Website: *www.elizabethchristies.com*
Facebook: *www.facebook.com/elizabethchristies*
Linkedin: *www.linkedin.com/in/elizabeth-christies-090b7a217*

JESSICA TRUEBLOOD

20 YEARS TO TAKE A HINT

In December of 2020 I paid off $30,000 worth of student loans from my Master's degree, an amount I had been paying monthly for 14 years. Four months later, I left my corporate career forever. The irony was not lost on me: I no longer felt obligated to stay in the career I had spent so much money and time on once that debt was paid.

How did this happen? How did a 20-year corporate grind end abruptly in 2021?

Looking back now, I see that there were several events in my life that were clues I needed to leave the corporate world, but none of them got my attention until 2021. In fact, there were four major hints.

I started working in the early 2000s. Since then, I've probably worked at 15 different companies – engineering firms, banks, nonprofits, healthcare companies, veterinary medicine, state government. Each was a slightly different version of the last.

My first full-time job after college was a disaster. I cried in the ladies' room at lunch every day for two weeks when I first started. A knot in my stomach would rise each day when the office park came into view as I crested that last hill. Weekends were a short respite, only to be cast aside each Sunday at 5pm when anxiety crept up slowly as the afternoon sunlight faded in my living room. I called it the Sunday Scaries.

Working in "corporate America" was nothing like the work I had glamorized from movies and television. What I found was a small, dark office with musty outdated furniture. On my first day I was shown to my "desk", which was a glorified folding table and an aging desktop computer.

I would call my parents and sob, secretly looking for permission to quit. I was 24, I didn't need anyone's permission, so why did I feel so guilty? I had a job; I should be thankful. I had health insurance and a regular paycheck. My parents, raised in a different generation, had little sympathy for me. "This is your life," my dad said. "It's not so bad, you'll see."

One evening I finally talked to a good friend who had been my roommate in college. She knew she wanted to be a teacher at age seven, and made a direct line for that career, never wavering. She told me to get over it, "This is what adults do. They work."

So I did what many young people do. I "got over it." I stopped crying. I got up in the dark, dressed for work and drove to an office for the next 20 years. I took my two weeks' vacation each year. I lamented with my friends about how we all hated our jobs.

Hint #1

The first time I really questioned a corporate lifestyle was when I was newly out of graduate school in 2007. I was working for a large aviation company. The economy was struggling and many of my friends suddenly found themselves unemployed. I was told my job was secure and was even asked to help put together severance letters and packets for the company's exiting employees.

What I didn't know at the time was that corporates don't owe you their loyalty. You work, they pay you, and that continues until one party decides to end that agreement. But as I said, I didn't know that in 2007. Imagine my surprise when I found myself looking at a severance packet with my name on it (that I had designed!) and being told, "Best of luck in your future endeavors!"

The months that followed were surprisingly happy for me. I found freelance work, and while I didn't have a lot of extra money that summer, I had enough.

Eventually I found another full-time job because that's what we're supposed to do, right? I needed stability and health insurance. And I went right back to the Sunday Scaries too.

Hint #2

In 2015, when I was pregnant with my son, I was traveling every other week, on my feet all day doing training classes and getting rave performance reviews. I felt invincible. I enjoyed my job and felt like I was making a real difference for a change.

I can only describe what happened next as a complete mental breakdown. Perinatal Anxiety and depression crept up while I was not looking, slid its claws around me at 33 weeks pregnant and didn't let go until my son was about four months old. I went from superwoman to someone who could barely get out of bed, who hardly slept, who ate only to nourish her baby.

I felt too ashamed to tell my manager what was happening, especially when I didn't understand it myself yet. I missed meetings and deadlines; I was a terrible employee.

While on maternity leave (only 12 weeks in the US), I found a therapist and some medication and started to heal. All too soon the Sunday Scaries were back, and I steeled myself to go back to work, because that's what we're supposed to do, right?

I soon learned that the working mom struggle was like nothing I had experienced before. From then on, I would be judged for returning to work, for nursing during the day, for bringing my pump and equipment to the airport when traveling for work. I was asked, "Who is taking care of your baby while you are gone?" and "I don't know how you leave your child. I could never."

The guilt was terrible in those years when my son was small. Do I take a promotion with more hours? Should I stay with a job I hate because it has better family medical coverage? Can we find a daycare with longer hours so that we can get to work on time?

There were a few fleeting moments when I wondered why there weren't more options for working mothers like me. Pushing those thoughts aside, I navigated the rocky toddler years with earaches, work meetings, sippy cups and wrinkle-free pantsuits.

Hint #3

In 2019 I applied for a new job. I was (again) burned out with the demands of a corporate job and motherhood and hoped a new company would be different. After 20 years of making these same decisions, I was growing weary of job changing but I did not have any other ideas. Self-employment was not yet in my vocabulary! This job would be different though, surely! A Director-level role with a nonprofit was just the thing to re-engage professional passion that was long gone! A big office and a larger salary, yes!

Two weeks into my new role I found out my sweet, vibrant and otherwise healthy mom had an aggressive and terminal cancer. Nothing else mattered from that moment until she passed away three short months later. My heart and mind were simply elsewhere. My employer was very supportive, to an extent. I had no time off due yet as a new employee, and my bereavement leave was only five days. There were many more days when I would get dressed for work, take my son to daycare and then drive myself home and sit on the couch crying. I missed deadlines and struggled to do the bare minimum.

We needed my income, so I managed to work as much as I could, because that's what we're supposed to do, right?

For the first time in my career, I had thoughts of leaving my job. I no longer felt that I was doing the right thing for myself or my family. After seeing cancer and death, my priorities were shifting. A title and a fancy office felt superficial compared to freedom, flexibility and autonomy.

In November 2019, the holidays looming, my husband suggested a hobby would occupy the time. I felt like small pieces of my personality were uncoiling, stretching out and pushing their way to the surface like plant roots. For the first time in months I felt happy and hopeful.

I started making Christmas ornaments. At first for friends and family, and then with my husband's encouragement I decided to attend a couple of craft shows. While the money from those holiday sales wasn't enough to replace my income, it lit the fire inside of me again. Simply put, creating made me happy. Motivational speakers tell you to find something you love and try to make a living at it, because then you'll never work a day in your life. Making a living from crafting, though?

Holiday ornaments don't sell well in January, unfortunately, so my plan had some limitations. As I brainstormed ways to sell my handmade products, it hit me … Etsy! Etsy is a marketplace for handmade products, and fortunately for me I already had a shop that was started in 2018 for fun but was completely unsuccessful. In fact, after my mother's diagnosis in 2019, I abandoned my shop. It was still technically open, but no products were selling. With fear and a tad of optimism, in January 2020 I re-opened my shop.

With a newfound passion for creating, it wasn't long before my old, but new, Etsy shop was filled with new listings, handmade wooden ornaments, magnets, and jewelry. Within a year, True Life Concepts had 900 sales. More importantly, I was excited about working and optimistic about the future.

While not enough income to leave my job, the Etsy shop was an adequate side business for a while, which was a nice distraction. Around that time, I started a Facebook group, **Etsy Underachievers**. Teaching has always been a passion of mine, and this group was a whole new way to share that passion with others. **Underachievers PLUS**, the coaching and training membership group launched in fall 2020, about nine months after the group was formed. For a small monthly charge, Etsy sellers now had access to over 50 hours of my training materials, worksheets, videos and a panel of business experts. After one year of the PLUS group, I was able to help 1000 Etsy sellers by combining my passion for teaching with my passion for Etsy!

Hint #4

After six months of 18-hour days, working my full-time job, being a mom and then working my two side hustles at night, something finally got my attention. After years of ignoring the various hints and signs about my career being unfulfilling, the pandemic blasted onto the scene and turned my world (and everyone else's) upside down.

Working from home was something I was already doing before the pandemic. In addition to all the things already on my plate, I now had my son at home all day. We were navigating kindergarten virtually while I struggled to be a good manager, wife, and small business owner all at the same time.

I finally said enough. And I took control of my life.

Paying off my student loan wasn't just about seeing the balance go to zero, it was so much more. I was finally free. My Etsy shop and my new coaching business were doing well and growing every month. After a lengthy conversation with my husband, I worked up the nerve to turn in my resignation.

I wish I could say that the rest is history. It took me months to resign from my job. In 2021, four months after I paid off the balance on my student loans I resigned. During those four months, I grew my Etsy shop, the Underachievers group, as well as my coaching business to match my corporate income. I worked long hours. I saved six months of revenue in my account for a safety net. I planned and agonized over the plan for months. I didn't really make a "leap" as some say, more like a calculated safe jump when the time was right!

My Facebook group now has 23,000 members, and my membership group has 500 paid members each month! Now when I need a mental health day, I take one. When my son is off school, I can be with him. But if I have a dip in revenue one month, it's all on me. The trade-off is worth it.

If you are reading this book, and feeling stuck, and have many hints of your own, take some time to reflect. Leaving your job may be more reachable than you think! Don't give up, even if it takes you 20 years to finally get the hint like I did!

ABOUT THE AUTHOR
JESSICA TRUEBLOOD

Jessica Trueblood is the founder of Etsy Underachievers, and the CEO of her company, Shop Review Crew.

She works with Etsy shop owners all over the world who want to create a sustainable and profitable business. Her specialty is teaching Etsy best practices, and she focuses on eliminating myths and false information often found online about selling on Etsy.

She also works with coaches who are struggling to grow their Facebook communities, and those who want to drop out of corporate jobs for the entrepreneurial life.

She has a Master of Education and 15 years teaching and training experience. She resides in Colorado, USA, with her husband and son. When she isn't talking about entrepreneurship, you can find her in the mountains with her family, or at the craft store.

You can connect with Jessica at *www.shopreviewcrew.com* or *www.happycorporatedropouts.com*

Instagram: *www.instagram.com/etsy_underachievers*

LinkedIn: *www.linkedin.com/in/jessica-trueblood*

LANA IVANOV

THE UNTOLD MINDSET OF THE AMERICAN DREAM

I was in my early twenties, a single mom and immigrant to the United States. I spoke very little English but somehow landed a job in a factory making $7.00/hr. It was my first day. I didn't sleep the night before, whether it was stress or nerves, it didn't matter. I was up at 5am, settling everything for my daughter's care before walking to the bus stop in the dead of winter in Massachusetts. It was a 20-minute walk, and each minute was filled with new questions, "How did I get to this point in my life?", "How am I going to take care of myself and my daughter?", "Where am I going to sleep tonight?", "Will I have enough money for food today?"

I finally arrived at the bus stop where a few people were waiting. The wind was slicing across my poorly covered skin. I got on the bus, sat down in silence and looked out the window for a few minutes. This was the bus to the factories. I looked around at the people riding with me. They were all tired, cold and old. They were easily between 50 to 70 years old. All I could think was, "Is this going to be my life? Is this what I have to look forward to?" It was the same bus every morning and evening, and the same tired, long faces to and from the factory, making $7.00/hr. to continue to struggle. I knew on that first bus ride that I wouldn't let myself turn into that. I wouldn't accept the situation I was in and let it control my career and life path. Those faces have been part of my success, the driving force behind so many decisions I've chosen professionally.

I grew up in Kazakhstan, Russia. I was the youngest of a very family-oriented and hard-working family. My parents were both professionals. My dad was an engineer and my mom was a director of a big fashion company, working in the corporate world. Her life was filled with fashion, jewelry and all the beautiful things. I was a bit of a surprise for my parents as my mom had me at 40 and my brother and sister were 11 and 18 years older than me. I grew up in the city; I had all the fast-paced glamorous city life a girl could have until my dad passed away when I was 11. My life dramatically changed. My dad was the main breadwinner, so we could no longer afford our beautiful condo and the city lifestyle and moved outside the city to a farm. My mom decided to stay home and work the farm.

We had many animals and a big garden. She was ultimately exhausted and in grief. She lived off her pension of $500/month. Until I was 18, I also had a "loss of father" pension for $400/month that was added to our income. We worked really hard. My mom became a beekeeper. To make money she'd collect honey from the field to sell in the winter. It was a laborious effort on both our parts to keep the farm and everything else running.

In my teenage years, I met a young man I enjoyed spending time with. We were friends at first and eventually started dating. His family had applied to emigrate to the United States of America when we were 17. I remember the day they had an interview in Moscow and he came to my house excited but determined not to live without me. He vowed that if they got the permission to emigrate, he wanted to marry me so I could go with them. They did indeed end up getting the invite and we were married. We had a big fancy wedding and ceremony in our local church when I was 17 years old.

A year later, I had my first daughter and, when she was nine months old, we were on our way to start our new life in the USA. I had a sense of guilt leaving my mom but I was so excited for the chance to create such huge opportunities for my family and children. I only knew of America from magazines or the movies. Everything I saw was always beautiful, big, shiny and successful. It was going to be this land of beauty and opportunity to do anything or become anything I ever wanted. We were both so excited to finally come to this big country to build our life together, the American Dream.

After arriving, I quickly realized how overwhelmed I was by the language, the life, the fast-paced feeling of being a foreigner and feeling completely stuck at the same time. It was not the picture I had painted in my head of what life would be like in the USA. We lived in Massachusetts. It was cold and gloomy. Life was tough. My husband began to work in the factory for very little money. He was not adapting to our new life well at all. He was depressed and started drinking heavily on a daily basis. He slowly became violent toward people and eventually his rage turned toward me. He was angry when he drank, and I became his source of anger. I would so often try to protect my daughter from witnessing his aggression but it turned into a daily activity. Some days he would just hit me, and I accepted and appreciated those days. Other days, he would give me a black eye, and crack my ribs. Those were harder days to accept. I felt stuck. I was in a new country with a young child. I didn't speak the language. I didn't have a job. What was I to do?

This went on for almost a year until one day he put me in hospital. He was angry, feeling defeated from work, feeling that he was not capable of reaching the opportunities he had dreamt of before we immigrated. He had been drinking heavily and came home enraged. I don't remember what specifically I did to set him off. It could have been the wrong meal choice or even a simple look, but he turned his anger toward me. He broke my nose, broke my ribs, held me by my throat and beat and bruised me with his hands and feet. The violence didn't stop until I was no longer able to move. I was in pain for days. I developed a cough, and every time I coughed, I had a sharp pain throughout my rib cage flowing around my body. I couldn't take a full breath without crying in pain. I went to the hospital where they determined I had pneumonia. It was the dead of summer; there was no reason for me to have pneumonia. They also realized I had a completely broken nose, and two cracked ribs, a damaged kidney and my jaw was knocked out of place. The doctors and nurses asked how this happened. I was afraid to tell them what I was going through so I lied. However, I left hospital, asking myself what he would do next or if I would even survive the next time. A few days later, my daughter was staying at her grandparent's house and he had another episode. When he was finished with me, he fell asleep and I ran out the door to my friend's house, bleeding and screaming. My friend drove me back to my house to help me retrieve my things. I was so scared. As I was getting my few belongings together, my husband began to fight my friend. I watched terrified, knowing he would likely kill me when he was done. However, my friend returned blow for blow and beat him up. I stood there looking at him, as he was finally the one sitting beat up. I remember telling him, "You are such a big brave guy, and you can only fight a woman who cannot defend herself." I went to the police station, filed a report and he was arrested. I was now officially starting from scratch.

I pulled myself together and decided to leave. I was basically homeless for a few months, bouncing around from friend to friend, sleeping on their couches. I stayed at the homeless shelter some nights and even a couple of nights in the park by myself. I often lay at night thinking of my mother, my father and my daughter. My mother used to say she knew I would be okay because she had always prayed for me, but here I was sitting in a dark hole. I had to figure something out. I would wonder how my life got to this place. I felt like a failure but also knew I wasn't afraid to work hard. I had a best friend, who is now my husband, who was helping me try to get my life in order. I got the job at the factory, and although it wasn't much, I was grateful for the opportunity to work. Those cold mornings on the bus to the factory were such important times for me to really start to imagine not only where I wanted to be but also where I didn't want to be.

I worked a greasy, dirty job on the factory line making parts for Volvo cars. I would be on my feet all day, not understanding the language and the culture, even having to ask if I could take five minutes to use the restroom. I remember walking by the offices and seeing the women who worked in there. They wore high heels, pretty dresses and made more money. I wanted that job. My husband and I started saving money, doing double shifts and eventually bought our first car. It was a very used Buick with four different colored doors, but it was ours and got me off the bus and one step closer to making a change for myself. I was so happy. I found myself pregnant with my son shortly after and with the support of my husband enrolled in college to learn English. I continued to work at the factory but knew after I learned English and got my associates degree, I would work in an office. Not long after graduating, I got hired at an insurance company. I felt so important. I was literally floating on cloud nine the first year.

My feet were not on the ground. I was making $15/hour and felt like I was finally on the right path to become a businesswoman. They used to call me the Russian ginger butterfly. I was always flying around, trying to help people, doing my absolute best at any task I was given, which meant I was soon doing three times the work of everyone else. I knew my job at the insurance company would be a career that would give me stability but I started to wonder about freedom. After a while, and many attempts to get a raise that would match my workload, I started to notice the situations around me. There were two women, Sandy and Karen, who I credit giving me the push I needed to step out of the corporate world and pursue my own path. They had both been with the company between 20 and 30 years so had great stability and a pension, a two-week paid vacation every year but were the most miserable people I have ever met in my life. They were on my team and every day we had the same conversation – how much they hated their jobs, how awful working there was, how they needed anti-depressants to get through the day. After speaking with them for ten minutes at a time, I would feel like I also needed anti-depressants, I would be so confused. They were American, they had no hang-ups. I would tell them, "If you hate your job, leave, start something new. YOU can do anything." They would just scoff and ask what's the purpose. I started to see they were not unique.

With every raise or title I got with the company, it was the same sentiment. People were exhausted, unhappy and basically just waiting to die. I also started to feel like I was going nowhere in my career. I was wasting my time, dragging myself there in the mornings and watching the clock to leave until I retired. I reminded myself of the faces on the bus. Even though I was no longer physically on the bus, I was there mentally and emotionally. I realized that 80 percent of my life was spent at work and if I hated what I did, then what was the real purpose of the job. It wasn't until my last review with my manager going over my performance that she suggested I take up the company counselling and get on anti-depressants to help me do my job better. I took her up on it but within six months I still felt the same way. I wasn't depressed; I just hated my job and environment.

I continued seeing the counsellor who urged me to consider a career where I help people and feel good about my work. I decided to go to nursing school. I still worked at the investment company while in nursing school and had my third baby, which was very difficult, but I was determined to create a better situation without putting my family under financial strain. I had a plan and that was the hope I needed to continue. There were times I wanted to quit but my husband and mother continued cheering me on. I graduated, left the investment company and started working at a hospital. I loved it. I felt like I was making an impact and helping people in their time of need, in their time of joy, in their time of grief. Whatever their circumstances, I was able to help them. I enjoyed my work, my family and friends and I was content.

One Friday afternoon when I was getting a facial, my aesthetician told me that she needed to step away from her job and sell her place. She needed surgery, her hands hurt, she was exhausted and needed to focus on herself.

I remember lying there and saying, "Wow, I wish I had your problem. You have the coolest job; I wish I could do this."

She quickly chimed in with, "Oh my gosh, you totally could do this!"

I said, "Okay, sure!" as a joke, but she was serious. She told me of all the possibilities. It was laid out in a way that was very easy to understand and exciting. I told her I would think about it over the weekend. She called me on the Saturday and we discussed it in more detail.

I then told my husband about it. He thought I was crazy. He thought I was having a midlife crisis but there was one aspect of the job that I couldn't get away from – the idea of making the world beautiful and happy, of making someone feel confident and good about themselves with something as simple as rejuvenating their skin. I loved it. I wanted to be a part of that world. I dragged my husband to the location on Sunday, talked more about it and agreed on a price. On Monday, we bought the place. Within four days, I had changed my mind and gone on a new career path. We agreed the woman we bought it from would continue to work for me until I got my license and felt comfortable with the processes.

It is the best decision I have ever made in my career life. It took me six months to get fully licensed. I didn't know much in the beginning but I was learning. The first few years were trial and error. I switched locations to attract a different clientele but ended up closing that location and teamed up with doctors to learn from, invested in a lot of education and training in lasers, derma technologies and so forth. At one point, I was so much in the red, I felt like I wouldn't succeed. However, with the continued work and striving to be among the best in the industry, in 2018 I opened my own place again: Advanced Aesthetics Medi Spa.

By now I knew how to run the business. I have a team of professionals working for me, bringing in six figures and making a difference in the lives of our clients. Over the years I saw so many women who lacked the confidence needed in life and business to reach out toward their dreams. I'm inspired and seek to provide that to my clients. I often think of those faces on the bus and wish I had been confidant enough at the time to tell them to take a chance, to do something great for themselves.

I think of myself, a girl who was brave enough to move to a new country, to leave an abusive relationship, to start a life while striving to succeed. I want to be what that girl needed, a mentor, a coach, someone saying, "You are enough. You can do this. You matter."

Now I can offer the right mindset and business coaching to women, encouraging them at whatever age or stage in their life they are or profession they have to be confident in who they are. I am a doer not a talker, and that separated me from so many people in the corporate world. I no longer wait for 5 o'clock to start living life. I have since even formulated my own medical grade skin care line and advanced facial protocol that is supplied to spas, doctors and dermatologists nationwide.

"Our deepest fear is not that we are inadequate. Our deepest fear is that we are powerful beyond measure. It is our light, not our darkness that most frightens us. We ask ourselves, 'Who am I to be brilliant, gorgeous, talented, fabulous?' Actually, who are you not to be? Your playing small does not serve the world. There is nothing enlightened about shrinking so that other people won't feel insecure around you. We are all meant to shine, as children do. And as we let our own light shine, we unconsciously give other people permission to do the same. As we are liberated from our own fear, our presence automatically liberates others." **Marianne Williamson** A Return to Love: Reflections on the principles of a course in miracles

ABOUT THE AUTHOR
LANA IVANOV

Mindset & Aesthetic Business Coach

Lana's passion in life has always been women's empowerment and personal development which she takes to a new level with her coaching. Her coaching program was specifically engineered for high-achieving women and spa owners who seek extraordinary results and want more.

She is an expert in the aesthetics industry, CEO and Owner of the award winning Advanced Aesthetic Medi Spa, RN, Medical Aesthetician, Microblading Artist, founder and formulator of Vonavi Pro Advanced Formulation skincare, entrepreneur and Confidence, Mindset and Aesthetic Business coach. Lana didn't just create a company; she created an industry.

Now she has been successfully coaching women to gain confidence through complete mindset transformation and to practice self-love, establish healthy beliefs and life habits and how to successfully grow their lives, careers and businesses. Lana's passion has always been to empower women through their self-development, to inspire their passions, to do what they love, as well as for Spa business owners to discover the foundational business techniques to achieve financial success beyond billable hours so that they can create a healthy work-life balance. Lana teaches her clients how to achieve overall equilibrium while growing beyond the $100k mark.

Email: *coach@lanaivanov.com*
Website 1: *www.lanaivanov.com*
Website 2: *www.vonavipro.com*
Phone: *413-210-3502*
Instagram: *www.instagram.com/lana_confidence_mindset_coach*
Facebook: *www.facebook.com/yelena.ivanov.94*

MARY GIRISHAA

IT WAS NEVER ABOUT THE MONEY

When I see other people take steps in life that I feel I could never take, I usually think they are either brave or lucky. I know my journey over the last 20 years can also look that way. It hasn't felt like either of those things though. Looking back, the pivotal moments on my squiggly life path have been the moments I connected with, listened to, and trusted my Truth. Or you could simply say I followed my heart.

Yes, I know, it sounds trite. Regardless, it's the best way I can describe a journey that was completely unexpected and saw me transition from Human Resource (HR) Executive to Ayurvedic Consultant and Yoga Teacher.

When I began my Ayurvedic studies in 2004 I was 45 years old and had been in HR Management for over 20 years. The wisdom of this ancient tradition drew me in even though I had never previously encountered or engaged with anything that could be described as 'alternate'. From the moment I opened a book titled *Absolute Beauty*, a birthday gift from my daughter, I was curious to know more. The same thing happened with Yoga a few years later.

As I went down the rabbit hole I knew this was how I wanted to live my life and, even though I began my studies with no intention of seeing clients or setting up a practice, sharing it with others was a natural progression. My exodus from the corporate world therefore wasn't so much a 'career' move, as a 'life' move.

When I look back at that time and those choices, I know that I wasn't thinking about the future and what felt safe. It was about what felt right in that moment. I had left my marriage six years earlier with very little materially because I didn't want to disrupt my children's life by halving the assets. I anticipated always having a well-paid job and I lived very simply. You know what they say about plans though ... When I handed back my company car, laptop and mobile phone in May 2007 I had just enough money in the bank to replace them and set up a little clinic space in my rented home. My shingle was up.

It's been over 14 years since I received that last payslip. It's also been 14 years since I paid tax. So it's obvious that the journey has never been about the money. However, I do want to assure you that I don't believe that there is anything spiritual about not having money. Money in the hands of good people does good things. Paying no tax is not as bad as it sounds though. I live what I do, so almost everything is a tax deduction. Money has just never been something that has overly influenced my decisions. There is a part of me that simply trusts I will always have what I need – enough to eat, clothes to wear and somewhere to live.

I can recall the first time I acted from this place of intuitivetrust. It was also the moment which marked the beginning of the end of my corporate life, although it was another 16 years before I finally closed the door.

Let me put this in context for you.

- It was September 1991; I was 32 and the main breadwinner for my family. My husband was a stay-at-home Dad with our three young daughters.

- This was my first day back after four weeks holiday, my first break for longer than a week in over three years.

- I had spent the last three years on a team commissioning and opening a new 500-bed teaching hospital and now headed up the HR Department with a team of 10 staff and over 2000 people on the payroll.

- A few months after we opened, a state-wide public sector financial crisis was announced. The knives came out as the end of the financial year loomed and two other local hospitals were earmarked for closure.

I returned from leave to find a hand-drawn organisational chart of the HR Department on the whiteboard in my office. Written underneath was an instruction to reduce one position. The HR department needed to downsize. *Hmm ... that's going to be interesting,* I thought.

Next came a phone call to meet with the Director of Corporate Services and the new CEO. I sat down with more than a little trepidation, sensing that what was coming wasn't going to be good.

With no preamble they told me my first task was to convince 200 people that redundancy was a preferable option to retrenchment. *No way, José* and *Do your own dirty work* came immediately to mind.

I walked back to my desk feeling numb and reflecting on the last three years. I thought about the team I had worked so tirelessly with and our excitement and pride at the opening ceremony earlier this year. I also thought about all the staff I had encouraged to be here. I felt completely gutted.

I had heard the news about the closures before I went on leave so I knew redundancies were imminent. What I didn't expect was what I experienced when I walked back in that first morning. The energy was heavy like quicksand, everyone's eyes were down, and it felt horrible. At the time I had no idea what that meant. In hindsight I realise I felt like the proverbial frog dropped into hot water.

Let me explain.

If you take a frog in its pond water and slowly heat the water, the frog doesn't notice the rising temperature and will stay in the water and slowly boil to death. However, if you heat the water to boiling point and then drop the frog in, it will jump straight out.

What I experienced that morning would have felt 'normal' if I hadn't had that time away. The stark contrast between the hospital's energy and mine after four wonderful weeks with my family allowed me the clarity and the knowing, without a shadow of a doubt, that I had to get out – just like the frog!

I knew I could do what they wanted but I knew I wouldn't. By 11.00am I had filled out a redundancy form and left the building. HR had achieved its staffing reduction of one position – mine.

The feeling was so strong and felt so right that, despite being the sole breadwinner, I didn't even talk to my husband first. I just filled out that form and went home and told him what I had done. God love him, he didn't bat an eyelid.

As I write this now, I am still blown away. Who does that? It also makes me feel a bit bullet proof. If I can do that, I can do anything.

Although that wasn't the end of my HR career, it was the beginning of the end. It was the first time I can recall listening to and acting solely from my intuition. The same inner knowing that ultimately led me to, begin my Ayurveda studies and to walk away from being an employee after 29 years.

In the 16 years between leaving this position and my final exit, I went to university full time to do a combined HR/IR degree and had three more HR management roles, which, in terms of a career path, was a slow and perfect downhill run. I went from working full time and managing large teams to progressively smaller organisations finishing in a part-time solo role. Not your typical career path. In fact, I was never conscious of 'having' a career. Jobs just came along, or at least I thought they did!

That's the essence of the timeline and what I call my front-line story. Now for what was happening on a deeper level and the final tipping point for my corporate exodus.

It's 2000, I'm in my early 40s and on the surface my life looks like everything you could want it to be. I was married to a wonderful man, we had three beautiful daughters, well-paid jobs, a wonderful home and no financial issues.

On the other side of the coin, years of long days and often bringing work home were taking their toll. I was also burning the candle at both ends with early mornings at the gym, keeping the house immaculate, and running around after three teenage daughters whose hormones were all over the place.

I lived life on the run. On one hand I was proud of how well I managed my never-ending to-do list and on the other completely exhausted and not knowing how to stop. I was a 'high achiever' and the messages I learnt in childhood about how important it was to be successful and look good were on constant replay. Dropping the ball felt out of the question.

Over time, home had become a battleground. I managed conflict with my daughters by yelling and screaming and medicating myself daily with red wine, bourbon and, on occasions, even marijuana. With the benefit of hindsight, I realise that I simply wasn't coping with life and had no idea what to do about that. I felt incredibly lost and empty and spent most of my time trying to desperately control everything around me to feel less overwhelmed by the chaos within.

Things began to both completely unravel and come together at the end of 2000. I was 41 and desperate for help. It came in the form of a flyer for a meditation course left on my desk at work. Saying I learnt to meditate sounds so simple and in no way captures the profound life-changing experience it was. I had always just done life, and now I was experiencing something that suggested that there was *more* to life than just doing it. I felt like I had found a part of me I had never known, but at the same time it also felt incredibly familiar.

Peace, love and light also sound trite, but the experience never is. Spiritual awakenings were simply not part of my world, but I had one.

Over the course of a week, on three separate occasions while meditating, I experienced a surge of energy in my third eye. Now, over 21 years later, I can count the number of times on one hand that I have drunk alcohol or eaten meat. I also haven't smoked (cigarettes or pot), worn make-up or dyed my hair. I can honestly say I have no sense of choosing to give anything up, nor have I had a moment's desire for any of them since. It was more like they gave me up – as if I'd put down the mask I'd been holding up for years because I no longer needed it.

As my meditation practice deepened, my awareness of my own 'stuff' expanded. Life became more about learning and growing. Exploring and peeling back the layers to discover who I wanted to be and how I wanted to live. I was officially on a 'journey', and this became the tipping point to leaving the corporate world.

The woman sitting across from me blew her nose and wiped her eyes. She was in trouble with her manager, and we had been here before, a few times. She was on my 'high maintenance' list and fast becoming the bane of her manager's life. I knew that she had no idea of what was really going on for her and if things kept going she was heading for dismissal.

More than anything I wanted to have a conversation with her about the patterns I could see playing out. I wanted to empower her to shift out of the victim mode she was stuck in, the place where "it was everyone else's fault". I wanted to help her open to the possibility of seeing this as an opportunity to shift the limiting beliefs that just weren't working for her and accept responsibility for the patterns playing out in her life.

My HR role however was about following the policies and procedures and ensuring I could defend any decisions in the Industrial Commission. Basically, covering the organisation's butt. The more I explored my own world and journey, the harder I found it to work within these limitations and the underlying adversarial nature of HR.

Another occasion that tipped my hand was during an Executive meeting. I was putting forward a proposal to engage one group of consultants over another and I can still clearly see the sneer on the Finance

Manager's face when I said that in addition to everything else, I intuitively felt that this was the right choice. To him the idea of using intuition to make a business decision was ludicrous and he made a point of telling me so in front of everyone.

The signposts were clearly telling me that this was no longer my world.

I knew I still wanted to work with people but in a different way. I wanted to share the understanding and skills I was developing on my own consciousness-raising journey to empower and inspire others. I wanted to help them wake up to their own power to heal and create a life that felt meaningful and purposeful. As it does, the Universe was conspiring in the background and, although I had never intended to practice Ayurveda, everything was perfectly aligned for the next step.

Towards the end of 2006 I had set up a practice space at home to complete the clinical assignments for my Ayurveda course. When they were all finished, many of the people I had been working with wanted to continue and were referring their friends and family. I had a practice if I wanted it, and I realised I did.

Fifteen years later I sometimes feel amazed at where I have landed, and the doors those moments of trust in myself and the Universe opened for me. I know now that whenever I follow my heart, wherever it takes me will be the right place, even if it sometimes takes me in a direction that wasn't part of 'my plan'. Which is why whenever I dream about or envision my future, I always add in the by-line *this or something better.* The outcome is a life that is completely different to anything I could have imagined.

I am so grateful that I didn't allow my limited imagination and fears of *not having enough* and *not being enough* to hijack my decision-making. That's not saying I didn't then, and don't now, experience those fears because, of course, I do. In those pivotal moments however, I've learnt not to allow them to have the final say. I know that a decision made from fear or insecurity, even with the best of intentions, is never aligned with my Truth, and will close rather than open doors.

Whenever I talk to my clients around what they're doing with their life and whether they feel fulfilled or have a sense of meaning or purpose, I share my experience with the intention of supporting them not to make decisions guided by fear or insecurity. One of my personal maxims is that it doesn't matter what you do, what is important is the reason or intention. You can do something for the right or wrong reason, and equally, not do it for the right or wrong reason.

The wrong reason is always related to fear. Like staying in a job that you know is slowly killing your spirit because you must pay the bills or saying no to something that pulls your heart because you are frighted it won't work. The right reason comes from listening to and trusting your Truth. Noticing when something feels completely off or lights you up and ignites your passion, and then following the signposts that the Universe provides to support you.

Which is another of my favourite maxims that I have come across in both spirituality and physics, that *energy follows attention*. When you give something your attention, energy flows in that direction. When we ask for things to change in our life, consciously or unconsciously, the creative universal energy conspires to help us.

I wasn't happy and knew something needed to change: I got a meditation course and a book; I loved what I discovered and did courses to learn more; what I learnt altered my perspective and priorities. Decisions that I would not have been able to make earlier came easily and signposts guided me to those things I would never have imagined. Twenty years later the journey has been incredibly rich and full: studying Ayurveda; becoming a Yoga teacher; living in an Ashram for three years; travelling the world as both a student and a teacher; and providing life-changing transformational programs for my clients.

When a part of you knows that something needs to change, notice what lights you up and begin to make it a part of your life. This lets the Universe know what you want and then it will conspire to help you.

Find and do what you love. It doesn't matter if it sounds trite. It's the Truth.

ABOUT THE AUTHOR
MARY GIRISHAA

Mary Girishaa is a Best-Selling Author and International Ayurveda and Yoga Teacher who supports women to reconnect and create a growth orientated relationship with themselves and life.

Her own conscious journey of discovery, beginning in her early 40's, has redesigned her and her life in a way that she could never have imagined. From Human Resource Executive to WellBeing Mentor and Guide, her studies and personal exploration of WellBeing over the last 20 years are the foundation of her unique transformational programme, *Conscious Transitions.*

This one-year life-changing journey supports women to create a whole new relationship with life; inspiring and empowering them to nurture and nourish themselves and navigate life more consciously, honouring their own Soul journey.

Mary Girishaa lives in Newcastle, NSW, Australia. She loves the beach, bike-riding, time in the kitchen and garden, and hanging out with her family, especially her six grandchildren.

Connect with Mary Girishaa at *www.2wisewomen.com.au*

Facebook Group: *www.facebook.com/groups/awarewellbeing*

MURIELLE MACHIELS

FROM OVERWORKED CEO
TO MEANINGFUL ENTREPRENEUR

If you're reading this book, it's probably because you're curious about making the jump toward being an entrepreneur. Is it a long-time dream? Has it popped up regularly in your mind? Or are you tired of having a boss and you want to be your own? But is being an entrepreneur for you?

Are you afraid of the uncertainties, the loneliness or getting enough money?

I want to share my story today from when I left my job as the CEO of a media company that had a staff of 130 people where I was making a lot of money to starting my own journey as an entrepreneur. I want to share the good, the bad, and the ugly because I think it matters that you get the whole picture before you decide whether you want to make this jump or not.

Let me start by telling you this: I have never regretted my decision. It wasn't an easy one to make for me because I'm pretty risk-averse, especially regarding money.

But today, unless I screw up badly, I would never want to go back to a corporate job. I love the freedom I have and I've built a life that I wouldn't even want to retire from.

In this chapter, I'll not only share my story but also how I carefully designed my new career and what I believe is the number one skill you need to develop if you'd also like to design your new life.

I'd like to start with this:

You are not on this planet to work like crazy for a paycheck.

You're not here to cross off items from the never-ending to-do list in your head. You're not here to run all the time with barely time to breathe, eat, exercise, or think. You're not on this planet to become numb, like a robot, day in and day out doing what others expect from you.

And you might think that you have no choice, but you have. You're much more powerful than you can possibly imagine. You can have a meaningful career with a great work-life balance **and** enough money to do and have the things you want.

You don't have to choose between having a career or having a great life with your family and friends. You can have both. But it requires a certain mindset and specific skills that I'll share in this chapter.

My name is Murielle Machiels. I'm the mother of two teenagers. Today, I'm an entrepreneur, a podcaster (Rebel Leader with a Heart), an academic Director, an MBA teacher, a writer, and a part-time digital nomad.

I've created *www.qileader.com* to help leaders build meaningful lives and organizations. I only work a couple of hours per day, and I travel a lot, at least two to three months a year.

My work is meaningful and I get to change people's lives.

I work mainly with large organizations and help them become more human-centered while increasing their impact.

The core of my business is an online program called "Leading authentically in digital times". I teach leaders the mindset, habits, and techniques needed to have more impact, more balance, and more meaning in this fast, uncertain and digital world. I also give keynotes and workshops.

The fear, sadness, and excitement of leaving my job as a CEO

I always knew that I would one day launch my own business. I had so many ideas but it was never the right time. My last corporate job was as a CEO in an educational publishing company.

I learned so many things about business, about people, about transformation, about private equity, about coaching but, most of all, about myself. It was the most challenging job I have ever had because we had to turn around the revenues, digitize it, go through acquisitions and reinvent the way we organize ourselves and do business.

But I loved the company. And at the same time, I hated the (lack of) values of my private equity shareholders. Of course, I made quite some money. One thing the private equity shareholders are very good at is "taking care" of the CEOs.

I had been a CEO for five years and launching my own business was all the time in the back of my head, like background music. When would be the right time to launch my business? I was convinced there would be a sign. What would be the sign? Would I see it? Could I maybe try to launch my business alongside my job? I tried but it was too hard. What could I launch? Would I become successful? Why would I leave this job? I love many things about it and it is financially safe. Would I regret quitting my job? I have a good life, why change it. These were all the stories that came with my background music until I knew the time was ripe.

I got several signs almost all at once! It felt like somebody was shouting: "Now is the time!!!"

So I first made a list of what gave me energy and what took energy in the work I was in. Then I looked at launching my new business, what would continue to give me energy, what might take energy and how could I mitigate the "energy eating" activities. I talked to my sister who encouraged me. Then I drafted a one-pager with my mission, customer target, value proposition, and competitive advantage.

96

I made an appointment with three good friends (and businesspeople) and asked if they thought I could be successful, what I needed to be careful about, how they could help me, what advice they could give me … I also talked to two people who had just launched their businesses to learn about their ups and downs. That was enough to make up my mind.

I made an appointment with my boss and resigned. It was a very rational decision and I was sure. I was very enthusiastic about my new life. But then, sadness and doubts kicked in. Have I made the wrong decision? My boss doesn't want me to leave, maybe he is right? And I cried. I cried a lot as if someone had died. Are the tears a sign that I made the wrong decision?

No, those were "mourning" tears because I was going to leave a company I partly built with my heart and soul for 12 years. It was like leaving a family that I loved and that loved me. And of course, the fear was there as well. Will I be successful? There are already so many offers in the market.

At other times, the enthusiasm kicked in with lots of ideas and lots of energy putting me back on track. Every time I overcame sadness or fear, it gave me more stability that I was on the right track.

I believe that getting out of your comfort zone to do something beautiful is like getting out of your chrysalis to become a butterfly. There is pain, fear, and sadness but you become a better version of yourself.

How did I find what to do?

Some of us are lucky and have found a passion early on in life. I wasn't among those people, I found mine by accident. In fact, my mess became my message.

An entrepreneur is often someone who finds a problem that other people face as well and develops a solution to that problem. And you often only need to be one step ahead, you don't have to be the expert from the start.

When I was the CEO of a media company, I was successful but I was also overworked.

At some point, I found myself at a crossroads:

- I could continue working hard but I could feel it would lead to a burnout
- I could change jobs, but I heard from others that it was the same in almost all organizations
- I could find a way to better deal with the fast, uncertain, and digital times.

And that's what I did. With trial and error, I found a way to lead the company with my heart and my head. And along the way, I had to transform myself as a leader and change my habits. It wasn't an easy road to success; it was full of challenges I had to overcome.

In the end, we achieved exceptional results in terms of profit and revenues. But most importantly, we had zero burnouts and an absenteeism half of the national average. People worked less and we had more impact.

That is what I teach to others today. My mess became my message.

The three questions I asked myself to design my new life

1. If I had all the money and competencies in the world, what would my life look like?

This is a very important question especially for someone like me who is very much influenced by the cult of achievement and always compares herself with the best in each area. Making money shouldn't become your main goal but only a means to an end. You quit your corporate job to lead a meaningful life, not to fall back into your old habits of working like crazy to simply make money. My answer to this question is this:

I want to help leaders build meaningful lives and organizations. I want to do that by working where and when I want, a maximum 30 hours per week, with a small team so that I have time to be with my family and friends, to exercise, eat healthy and travel around the world.

And today, I have reached exactly that.

2. How much money do I need to make to have that life?

It's important to do the math and to calculate how much money your new life and business would cost. What are my private costs (mortgage, groceries, kids, holidays …) and what are my business costs (accountant, employees, marketing, IT, office …)? I've estimated that I need to make €15.000 per month to pay myself and my team and have that life.

3. What will I offer to make that revenue in line with the life I want?

I decided to launch an online course combined with keynotes and workshops. This allows me to generate revenue and to work where I want. The automation and small team allow me to work 25–30 hours per week, mainly on things that give me energy. I slowly grew towards the revenue and the team. It took me two to three years to get there.

On *www.qileader.com/launchmybusiness you* can find a PDF to help you in launching your business.

**But there are already so many coaches, consultants, online courses …
How can I differentiate myself?**

That's the beauty of a world of abundance. On one hand, you can't be the only one with a certain offer anymore. There will be many. But when you're not alone in a niche, it means that there is a market for what you offer. So that's a good sign.

In a world of abundance and choice, people don't buy what you do, they buy why you do it. Your authentic self with your values is what sets you apart from others.

People buy from me because I am authentic, vulnerable, caring with a rebel side and strong. People follow me because I tell my story with the successful ending but also with all the raw and hard times. They can relate to me and find hope. If I managed to change from the same bad start situation as them, it means they could succeed as well.

Anxiety over future revenue is my biggest stress

When I look back at my business, I'm very proud and I see it growing more every year. But there are times of great anxiety.

In 2019, at the end of June I was making a €15K loss. So if my last six months were similar to the first six, it would mean I would lose €30K. In 2020, it was possible I would even make a €35K loss by the end of June.

I could feel a knot in my stomach, a compressed chest and that's when the negative thoughts appeared. "You are a failure. You're never going to make it. It's too hard, you must work harder. You're not good enough. Look at […] she made €1 million after one year. You should be further than where you are. You suck. You should quit. You're not an entrepreneur, let's face it. People think that you are successful but if they really knew."

But then, by sticking to my plan, trusting myself and my business, and pivoting after each failure, the business thrived during the last six months of each year. By the end of 2019, I ended up breaking-even while paying myself and two other people. And in 2020, we made an almost €40K profit on top of our salaries. And 2021 looks even better than 2020.

Overcoming my financial anxiety is my biggest challenge. This is how I do it.

As I told you in the beginning, I'm a very risk-averse person and I've read in a study that most successful entrepreneurs are risk-averse. So don't think you have to be willing to take a huge risk to become an entrepreneur.

These are the four steps I took to manage my financial anxiety. The last step is the most important one and the skill you need to develop whether you are an entrepreneur or an employee. This last skill has become my number one priority as a CEO and as an entrepreneur.

Step one: I built a financial safety net.

Before deciding to become an entrepreneur, I saved some money. I have enough money to survive one year without any revenue. That's a lot and I don't think you need as much. But for me, I feel somewhat safer to have that financial safety net.

On top of this, I know that if I need to, I can find a job very rapidly, especially at a lower level. I think it's important to write down for yourself, what the worst that can happen is. And if that happened, what are your options?

As a coach, I see over and over again that people are more afraid of what could happen, of what they imagine in their head, than of the actual situation. When they are faced with the actual big failure (a job loss, bankruptcy, a failed launch, a divorce …) they handle it pretty well. I'm not saying it's easy or nice, but they rise to the challenge.

Another great way to start can be to reduce your current hours and start your new business next to your current job. Then you can either slowly decrease one side or increase the other side (if possible). Or once you jump, you at least have a proof of concept or a basis to start from.

Step two: I work in iterations to minimize risks

I saw so many people start their own business by working on an expensive website, printing business cards, and developing a detailed offer. That's a very exciting time in your business. But then, once you are ready, the customers don't come and that's when you start to panic.

Trust me, that's not the way to start. I've made that mistake. Then I realized I had to start over. When I decided to launch my online course, I developed the course outline, a sales page, one module (out of six) and I sent one mail to explain the course.

Once I saw that people enrolled and paid for the course, I started building the other online modules. And then with every launch, I improved the course with the feedback from my customers.

You don't have to figure everything out in advance. In fact, that's often counterproductive. Just figure out the overall objective and your next step. My favorite quote nowadays is "Good enough for now, safe enough to continue".

Step three: I built partnerships

I started my business also to have more freedom, but at first I was very reluctant to partnering. I wanted to create my thing until I realized that together we're stronger.

Today I have my own business and partnerships. The first partnership I created was with a university, the best business school in Belgium. They didn't have any online course for executives, and I didn't have a brand or reputation yet. By partnering, we both grew our reputation and revenues. Then I formed partnerships with other coaches and consultants. We share projects, collaborate or sometimes simply talk and help each other.

I also joined a coworking office. It gives me a lot of energy to be surrounded by other entrepreneurs. They give me great ideas; we give each other feedback and support, which is very helpful. Because, you're going to have tough days. That's for sure.

But being an entrepreneur is about accepting those tough days; failing regularly but learning from it; finding the courage to get up and try again until you succeed.

That's why the next step is the most crucial one for me.

Step 4: Managing my energy is my number one priority

When my energy is low, my thoughts are negative, and I want to quit.

When I'm stressed or tired, I'm not creative and work hard for too little impact.

With low energy, I resist change and stay in my comfort zone instead of growing and overcoming challenges.

When I don't feel energized, I can't focus and get overworked.

When I feel bad, I become a firefighter instead of thinking strategically about the challenges I face.

In the last 10 years as a CEO and as an entrepreneur, I've realized that my number one job is to manage my energy. That's why I don't work that much. That's how I get great results with a wonderful work-life balance. That's how I implement things so much faster than bigger organizations.

If there is one skill you need to master as an entrepreneur it is this one: Learn to manage your energy very well.

It's because you have good energy and feel good that you'll have positive results. Too many people think it is the other way around: "When I have great results, then I'll feel good, and I will have time to stop."

And when you feel happy, you're open to learning new skills that will lead to more success. That's also when you have the energy to reinvent things because of a new social media algorithm, a new competitor, a disappointed customer, a big technological bug or another of the hundred challenges you'll face.

And when I feel good, I'm rarely anxious about my financial situation. I can surrender to whatever happens and see the situation as an opportunity to grow instead of a sign of failure.

Today, I love my new life as an entrepreneur, and I would never want to go back

It's not always easy but it is always meaningful, and I found ways to overcome my financial anxiety.

ABOUT THE AUTHOR
MURIELLE MACHIELS

Murielle Machiels is an entrepreneur, podcaster (Rebel Leader with a Heart), online course creator, academic director, MBA teacher and a mom. She and her small team do most of the work online and have automated most of the business. This allows her to have a lot of free time and to be a part-time digital nomad.

She helps leaders build meaningful lives and more human organizations.

Before starting her business QiLeader, she was the CEO of a media company that she transformed successfully for the digital times. She achieved great financial results, zero burnouts and 50% less absenteeism. But she encountered many challenges and almost burned out in the process. She had to transform herself to achieve impact, meaning and balance. Then she wanted to help other leaders achieve similar results.

You can connect with Murielle at: *www.qileader.com*

LinkedIn: *www.linkedin.com/in/murielle-machiels-ab09621*
Facebook: *www.facebook.com/Muriellemachiels*

Podcast: www.podcasts.apple.com/be/podcast/rebel-leader-with-a-heart/id1515882709

NANCY MCKAY

YOUR INNER WISDOM

"The best way to predict your future is to create it."
~ Abraham Lincoln

I was raised with the philosophy that you get a good job, work hard at that job and finally retire to live happily ever after. I did not believe in that philosophy. I was also raised in a highly functional alcoholic household where keeping up appearances was paramount. I learned at an early age the pattern of people-pleasing. This makes for a great employee, and for me, periods of deep unhappiness.

I began working in the oil and gas industry in the early 1980s. I was hired as the receptionist for a start-up company where I met and worked with some great people. They became like a second family. I worked my way into a position as a lease and rental analyst. It was a demanding and detail-oriented job and I was good at it. There was a lot of growth with the company for the first few years. The oil and gas industry is very volatile and, after several years, the bulk of the staff had been laid off. I managed to hold onto my job for five years.

I was reunited with several of my former colleagues at my next job. It was great. The company had the oil and gas division in Denver and a mining division in Fairbanks, Alaska. In 1987 the company relocated both offices to Vancouver, Washington. This was the first time that I would live out of the state of Colorado, and I was very excited. When the plane landed in Portland, I felt home for the first time in my life. I told myself I was never moving back to Colorado. I had a great time and I met and became friends with great people.

106

After being at this job for a couple of years, I grew very bored and decided I needed a change. My boyfriend at the time had introduced me to the art scene and I was smitten. I had also fallen in love with the Oregon coast. I set my intentions to work in a gallery on the coast. At lunch one Friday, I lamented to my dear friend Terri, and told her my plan. She was skeptical to say the least, but I don't recall being told to get my head out of my ass, so after lunch, I walked into my boss's office and told her I was quitting. She asked when, and I looked at my watch. After she regained her composure, she said she wanted to make sure HR would give me my job back when I came to my senses. I packed up my office and I was unemployed by 3:00 pm. This was the first time in my life I had left a job without having another to take its place. It was liberating and surprisingly not terrifying.

Over the weekend I made plans. I wrote a long letter to my parents explaining that I just couldn't keep doing this type of work and letting them know that even though I knew I was disappointing them, I had to do what I felt was right for me. Bright and early Monday morning I set out with enough résumés to last until I found a job. Starting at the north end of the coast and working my way south, I stopped at every art gallery along the way and I got a lot of rejections.

I pulled into Gleneden Beach, home of the Salishan Lodge, and walked into Maveety Gallery. I was offered a job as a bookkeeper. Now, math and certainly money, were not my strong suits but I loved this gallery and accepted the position. One of the women there knew of an apartment for rent so I made an appointment and signed a lease that day. Now it was back to Vancouver to pack up and move.

I worked at the art gallery for two years until my mom was diagnosed with lung cancer. I spent two weeks with my parents back in Denver, helping and supporting them as my mom underwent surgery to remove half of her left lung. During that time the three of us discussed my moving back to Denver. I experienced a tug-of-war; wanting to be close to my family and still wanting to live my life away from them. I was torn, and yet the *need to feel needed* won out. I contacted my friends in the oil and gas business to ask for help in finding a job. I was given a lead for a contract position as a lease analyst with a large, national firm. I was interviewed the day before I left Denver.

When I arrived back home in Oregon, and checked in with my parents, I learned the company called to offer me the job while I was still in the air. This was a very bittersweet moment for me. I broke the news to my boss over breakfast the next morning. We had really grown close and we were a good team. When it came time to leave the Oregon coast, I wasn't just leaving my friends and a job that I loved behind, I was leaving my heart as well. I felt defeated.

Spring of 1991 and I'm back in the oil business and living with my parents. I was 34 years old and I was determined to find an apartment as soon as possible. My now long-distance relationship didn't hold up either, and we parted ways, once and for all. Something deep inside me was reignited. The art bug bit me again. I began looking for a job in a gallery but couldn't find anything. I was growing weary of working for other people. I wanted to create my future. I decided to start my own art consulting business – I mean, why not? To say my parents objected to the idea is an understatement, and they offered very little emotional support. My father told me that I took after my great grandfather and had his entrepreneurial spirit. I believe there was a part of him that admired that trait, and yet he couldn't support it. I represented a few artists and I even quit my day job to be a cocktail waitress to support my dream, but it was an endeavor that never really took flight.

Reluctantly, I fell back on my experience in oil and gas and found a new position as a lease analyst in 1992. The work was tolerable and the best part was I working with great people. Once again, they turned out to be family. I had a *lot* of fun working and partying with them and they were there for me when my mom died in 1995. Also in 1995, I met Jimmy. I fell hard. I would look for any excuse to be near him. He liked me but he wasn't interested in being in a relationship. I continued the chase anyway.

I got laid off again in 1996. The company laid off so many employees that we qualified for the Trade Readjustment Act. The TRA provided unemployment benefits and allowed for up to two years of paid tuition to complete a degree that would lead to a new career. I chose Interior Design. I was in heaven. I loved everything about it – learning to draft, render (color), art history, textiles, everything.

In September of 1997, after reading a popular relationship book, I realized that I was behaving in a way that didn't serve me at all. I called Jimmy and told him the chase was over, that I hoped we could still be friends, but I was done. A couple of weeks later, he decided being in a relationship wasn't such a bad idea. One night, he pulled into the alley and invited me to go for a ride in his new car. We've been together ever since.

I landed a paid internship with a prestigious international architectural firm before I graduated in 1998. I was *way* out of my element and comfort zone. I tried like hell but came home and cried at the end of every day because of the pressure. I had my one and only panic attack while working for this company. A week after I received a $500 bonus and the day after Jimmy moved in, I was let go. I was devastated and relieved at the same time.

What does one do when you've received a confidence-crushing gut punch? Of course, you go back to what you know best, oil and gas, right? Because that's a sure thing – sure to make money and sure to make me miserable. Thankfully, it was brief and then I came to my senses and found a design tech position with a small kitchen and bath design firm the following January. I loved what I was doing, but not who I was doing it for.

After a year, I moved to another firm, one more well-known and respected. I enjoyed that, but the owner was a bit of an asshole, so after another year, I went down the street to an even more well known, respected and exclusive firm. I worked there for five years. During that time, I was working for one of the best, and most difficult, designers I'd ever known. She was an excellent designer and a demanding teacher. She challenged me. I loved that job, and I was good at it. So good, that I wasn't permitted to grow beyond being a design tech. I wanted to be a designer.

Once again, my inner voice and entrepreneurial spirit kicked in. I quit my job in 2006 and started my own kitchen and bath design business. Design Solutions was born. I had no idea what I was doing business wise, and I was determined to be successful. I worked hard and learned some very valuable lessons. I also worked with a small design firm part-time to hedge my bets.

ε♥

One beautiful Monday morning in March 2007, my father committed suicide. I found him dead in his bed, with pills and a bottle of unidentified alcohol on the nightstand. His battle with alcoholism and his endless grieving of my mother's death was over. Even though I knew he'd been drinking again, his death was a shock.

My guilt over his death escalated my drinking and my trip down the rabbit hole. Now, I was always a "party girl." I was mostly responsible (sort of). I never had any consequences from my drinking: no lost job, no DUI, no trips to the hospital.

I was working on a big project with my part-time gig at the time of my dad's death. The extraordinarily demanding client was kind and compassionate for a day or two, and then I saw that she simply didn't give a damn. If I couldn't produce what she wanted by the end of the following week, we would lose the job. After hundreds of hours of work, I simply couldn't cope with that too, and told the owner of the design studio I was done. For the next two years, I tried like hell to keep it together, but I was falling apart and I was using alcohol to cope and numb myself. My drinking was becoming very unpredictable.

Friday the thirteenth of March 2009 started off as usual, with a hangover, feeling nauseous and hands shaking so badly I could barely draw on my eyeliner. It ended with a failed suicide attempt that scared me sober. I realized I couldn't drink safely anymore.

I spent most of the next year working on my sobriety like it was a full-time job. I kept my toes in design, but the economy had taken a downturn and the custom home business was getting hit hard. About a year after I got sober and had spent the majority of my inheritance from my dad, Jimmy suggested I look for a *real* job in oil and gas. There it was *again.* Fuck.

Even though I had been out of the industry for 14 years, I started looking. I interviewed with the Land Admin Manager and the Senior Lease Analyst at the Denver office of a Canadian firm. I told them that even though I'd been out of the industry for 14 years, I would be an asset to their team. They recommended me for the position.

It was a great job, with a great company, and I was over the moon. The woman I was reporting to, Rhonda, was awesome. She was smart, funny, and easy to communicate with. I was so excited to work for her. My co-worker, Pat, was equally as impressive and was easy to learn from and relate to. To my dismay, Rhonda received a job offer that she couldn't refuse a couple of weeks after my start date, and she left shortly afterwards.

Rhonda was replaced by a woman who I will refer to as "Toxic", who could not come even remotely close to filling the shoes of her predecessor. Not only did she make promises she had no intention of keeping but was adept at two-faced behavior. During this time, she fit right in because company culture was declining rapidly. In one meeting I heard "we cheat to win". This is nowhere in the realm of my values and I was appalled. Between "Toxic" and the company culture in general, I started looking for work elsewhere. Finally, the president of US Operations, several senior managers, as well as "Toxic" were fired. The company finally realized that the US group needed to realign the culture.

Fortunately, her replacement, Sandi, was on par with my first supervisor. After she settled in, we discussed my dissatisfaction with the direction, or lack of it, that my career was taking. She knew and worked with people I had worked with in the past and she respected them. As a result, she respected me, valued me and my contributions to the department. She recommended me for a hard-earned promotion and a well-deserved salary increase, both of which were awarded to me. She went on to encourage me to grow professionally, even if it meant leaving her department.

I made a lateral move where there was more opportunity for future growth.

I worked hard and made my ambitions known to my leaders. I was promoted but not compensated according to the position. If I knew then what I know now … holy shit.

8♥

And then on my 58th birthday, I woke up after receiving a total hysterectomy to learn I had Stage 1C ovarian cancer. I was told I would start chemo before the end of the month.

The idea of chemo terrified me. In fact, I wasn't going to do it. I watched my mom go through it and a friend had died after an allergic reaction to chemo. And then one day, my intuition kicked in and I knew that everything would be okay. Still I was very scared for my first round. The nurses and Jimmy took great care of me and I didn't have any problems.

My infusions were scheduled for Wednesdays every three weeks. I had intended to have chemo, go to work on Thursday and Friday, feel like shit on Saturday and Sunday, and be back at work on Monday.

Then the fatigue struck. It reminded me of the saying, "If you want to make God laugh, make plans."

I never made it to work the day after, or even the Monday after, but a *week* from Monday after. It took me 10 days to recover after each round. Thankfully, and surprisingly, my boss and the company were understanding and supportive. I was still so tangled up in people-pleasing that I just knew I was letting everyone down and was putting my job in jeopardy.

A few months after I completed chemo, my energy started to return. Every month I felt better. I was carrying even *more* weight as a result of the chemo, but otherwise, I was healthy. I was clear. No evidence of disease.

And then, something interesting happened – *my perspective started to change.* By the beginning of the following year, I started feeling very unfulfilled at work. My mantra became **"I didn't get sober and survive cancer to be miserable."**

I was already in therapy and I started working with a life coach as well. Working with a life coach was so beneficial, even more so than therapy. Life coaching is all about focusing on the future rather than the past. We can't change what happened in our pasts, and we can only change how we move forward from where we are. I worked with another life coach a little while later and realized that this was something I wanted to do. I began creating my new career in 2017 at the age of 60, when most people are thinking about retiring. I'm now a Certified Mind-Body-Eating Coach, a Certified Wayfinder Life Coach and a Certified Equus Coach. I have found that working with horses alongside my clients is pure magic.

&❧

One of the lessons I've learned, as I look back on my life in general and over 40 years working in the corporate world, is this; *Listen to your inner wisdom.* We all have our truth inside of us. It usually takes assistance for us to uncover it, but it is *there.* When my inner wisdom told me to light the fire of entrepreneurship, I listened and, initially, gave up too easily, with both the art and design endeavors. It just wasn't the right time. There was more I needed to learn. I learned to dream big and listen to my intuition. Now, I'm thriving as a business owner. I love helping people transform their lives. To watch the light come back into their eyes is truly a privilege. It's never too late to create a life you love.

ABOUT THE AUTHOR
NANCY MCKAY

Nancy J. McKay is the founder of Amazing Outlook Coaching, LLC.

She is a Certified Life and Equus Coach® helping women who are over-drinking change their relationship with alcohol. Her mantra that created her new career was "I didn't get sober and survive cancer to be miserable."

Nancy works with her clients virtually, and with horses, to uncover the limiting beliefs that are keeping them stuck in the muck of unhealthy behaviours.

Nancy is a contributing author to two previous books; *Ready to Fly: Volume 3* and the international bestseller, *Phoenix Rising: Powerful Women Who Rose from The Ashes to Claim Their Place.* Nancy is also a frequent podcast guest and speaker, sharing her inspiring story of recovery and creating a new life after cancer.

Nancy lives in Lakewood, Colorado, with her husband and their two rescued Westies. You can connect with Nancy at *www.amazingoutlookcoaching.com*

Facebook: *www.facebook.com/nancy.mckay1*
Facebook Page: *www.facebook.com/amazingoutlookcoaching*
Linkedin: *www.linkedin.com/in/nancymckay*
Instagram: *www.instagram.com/recoverywithnancy*

PATRICIA LINDNER

BODY COMPASS TO ALIGNMENT

I vividly, and painfully, remember a Friday morning in April 2017. It was still early and the warmth of my bed didn't want to let me get up. Five more minutes and I could move my tired body to the bathroom and take a cool shower to fully wake up ... but that didn't happen that day as the sore stiffness and the tired heaviness of my muscles and joints held me back. The feeling I perceived was like a full body ache shackling me to the warmth of my blanket. There was no sense of cosiness at all – the blanket felt like an immense weight that I was unable to lift.

This forced me to listen and be in the moment. Time stood still. And I, the successful teacher's trainer in a well-paid leadership position, multitasking mom of two amazing kids and wife of a loving husband, needed to admit that it was high time to take a break. But my greatest desire was to quickly function again. I took sick leave and saw quite a lot of doctors in the next couple of weeks, expecting them to fix my problem. Needless to say that I didn't notice much progress with the pain in my body that felt very depressing and was weighing me down even more. It wasn't until I had a weird and very realistic dream one night, in which my dad, who had died three years earlier, told me that his occurring in my dream was a final warning and last opportunity to heal my body and start over again.

Why was it my dad that occurred in my dreams? Hadn't he always been one of my biggest cheerleaders to push forward and crawl up the career ladder? Hadn't he been so proud of his daughter's brilliant successes? This dream reminded me of all the outstanding milestones in the last decades and made me think of all my past accomplishments.

As far as I remember I had always been a very driven and determined person. A tough go-getter, fabulous organizer and high performer, hiding her extremely sensitive character behind intelligence, toughness and success. When I started working as a teacher in 1999 I naturally was one of the best graduates who was offered a special and additional training field next to working in a school class. I loved being responsible for interesting tasks and trainings. After only a couple of years I was asked to take on an additional job as an expert for teaching English and doing workshops for fellow teachers. What an honour! I was continually offered more responsible positions, even when I got pregnant in 2007. They relied on me and had these great expectations of a highly professional woman who certainly would find a way to be a mom and handle her responsibilities at work. And so I did. When my second child was born in 2010 I still tried to not compromise anything ... except my well-being.

Whenever my body asked for attention and told me that I was definitely overriding my natural cycles, I admit I chose the fastest and easiest road and swallowed painkillers. Then I went on doing what I was best at: taking care of my two babies and being highly professional at work. I also wanted to experience a harmonious, loving and "successful" marriage. Although the father of my two children tried to be as supportive as he could, there were so many unresolved issues on his side (and probably some also on mine) that we decided to break up when the kids were only two and four years old.

Looking back makes me remember that time of all those heavy burdens and painful events. Some years later my dad became very ill and was diagnosed with terminal cancer at only 69 years. Luckily I had met my current husband some time before that, so I received loving support during this difficult time. Driven and determined to succeed, I wanted to rescue my father by studying everything about alternative cancer treatment and healing. I wanted to do something to fix this. I really don't know how I managed studying alternative treatments and going to appointments with my dad while working as a successful teacher with quite a lot of additional tasks, raising my son and my daughter and clearing the last issues with my kids' dad.

117

Unfortunately my dad died in October 2014. A heavy and nagging thought that I carried around for quite some years after my father's death was, "I failed!" Despite all my efforts, the research and treatments I found out about, I finally couldn't help him. I guess that these thoughts and all the stressful events of the years before weakened my immune system, which meant I contracted the Epstein-Barr Virus a couple of month later. You don't have to second guess that I didn't take this infection as seriously as I should have. I simply was programmed to go, go, go! In spite of the aftermath of the viral infection, as the high-achieving woman I was, I even applied for a rare and amazing leadership position as a teacher's trainer in 2015.

It was such an honour, such a joy when I finally got to know that they really wanted me for this position. But there was also sadness mixed amongst the celebration of climbing the career ladder. Joy was accompanied by grief and disappointment because of my father's early death. A predominant thought at that time was, "If only he could witness this glorious success!"

This new job meant more responsibility, more influence and the opportunity to plant inspirational seeds in the young teachers' lives. I wanted to make an impact and change the system. I wanted to revolutionize education. I imagined big visions of an even bigger mission.

I really loved working with the young teachers, giving them feedback on their teaching style and providing them with wisdom, insights and ideas that went far outside what was expected. I absolutely enjoyed being their creative and free-spirited instigator. Besides working passionately in this job and taking care of my own kids, I consistently took apprenticeships in systemic coaching, ancestral healing work as well as creative and intuitive work, as I thought this background would increase my potential to change the crusted educational system.

Soon I needed to realize that I was sort of a bird of paradise in a big flock of blackbirds. Actually, I was headed in a completely different direction. All my intentions to bring change, openness and creativity failed badly. I was shown to be only a small figure in this game that was

118

played with strict and traditional rules. I was asked to adapt to the long-held values and accept what the system expected me to be like. More than that, the crusted, politically driven system leveraged my expertise wherever and whenever it could. I was talked into offering my experience and knowledge and to be of service for the system without really being seen, appreciated or getting a return on investment. And of course, without honouring my boundaries I was expected to function and to give more than I was capable of.

From time to time I had the vision of breaking free from this soul-sucking career. But as already mentioned, I loved working with the young adults and there was still a spark of hope for the change I imagined. At least I talked myself into this. Today I openly admit that I doubted so many things and mandatory tasks, but I didn't speak up, I didn't stop working in this position, I even adapted and felt safe in this comfort zone of pain. Why should I take any risks and leave the known? All in all it was something that was quite okay and safe. So I started telling myself stories about needing to be so grateful for everything I had. I shamed myself for complaining at such a high level and convinced myself that I needed to be proud of all the success and accomplishments. Other people even envied me because of my outstanding position and the money I earned. So why didn't I celebrate myself?

"Be happy with what you have, Patricia!" was my daily mantra. "Your dad would be proud of you!", a voice in my head that wanted to comfort me said. It is proven that if we tell ourselves a story long enough, we really start believing in it. The truth is that we absolutely are the co-creators of our current realities. And oftentimes we don't remember that we actually dreamed of something different. Interestingly, compromising ourselves becomes something that feels natural and we are convinced of not having a choice. The longer we accept the conditions and limitations the more they become our unshakeable reality. At least that's what it was like for me.

Believing in this false narrative was the reason for not paying attention to my gut. I tried to not hear this yearning for something I couldn't define. I also ignored early signs of pains and aches and not feeling well in my body. I simply numbed them all by being busy or by swallowing painkillers.

Back then I didn't know the immense power and wisdom of my body and soul. I always relied on my mind and my intelligence. Now I need to say that my body was my wise guide and compass into a new life. By producing more and more symptoms it caught my attention. Today I can't thank my wise body enough for what happened to me – or better, FOR me – on that Friday in April 2017 when I couldn't get up and function any longer.

In July 2017, I finally decided to take one year off without pay and embark on something I called "My Healing Journey." When you read this, it sounds like an easy thing, like deciding to go on a holiday. Believe me, it was nothing like that for me. I knew that I wasn't able to continue working for a while and that I needed to take care of my body and soul. But at the same time it felt like being a complete failure, a nobody, a loser. A weak woman! Darn! I didn't want to be perceived as weak! Who was I without my work, my title, my great income?

It took quite some months to get acquainted with the emptiness of how that actually felt - like restlessness inside me. I wanted to fill the days with something meaningful. I didn't want to take a break. So much internal masculine go-getter energy wanted me to function, achieve and do! And I wanted somebody to fix this ongoing, weird pain in my body.

As I had experienced a huge number of fabulous apprenticeships while still in my teaching career, I started offering my service to friends and acquaintances. I mainly did this to be of service and to do something to counter the boring and devastating emptiness. Soon these little jobs I did were not enough for me so I tried to fill my calendar with scheduled sessions for people who wanted to either get some guidance, gain clarity or go through a healing. I'm telling you about this phase as I want to share that my masculine high-achiever energy and the pattern of doing instead of being didn't disappear when leaving my amazing career. I was literally bound to this pattern. I was addicted to organizing, planning, multitasking and overriding body symptoms and natural cycles. But this was something I could not consciously stop.

When I discovered I did not know how to market myself, how to create a stunning website or how to create a potential business of my own, I felt like an absolute beginner. I started comparing myself with the icons in the market and couldn't stop criticizing myself for this lack. I wanted to be perfect in this newly discovered world. I wanted to learn from the experts in the least amount of time and become masterful in what I did. It then dawned on me that one year off was not enough. I needed to take another year off and dive into all the business knowledge that I lacked. I loved the challenge but I didn't feel much joy or bliss when studying the laws, rules and strategies that successful entrepreneurs recommended and taught. My eagerness forced me into learning. "If I want to become successful with a real business, I need to follow the exact steps they preach!" was my new affirmation on the road to living a healthy and happy life. Remember, I originally declared my year off as "My Healing Journey", which soon turned out to be an exact copy of what I had been doing in my previous career. Needless to say, my body symptoms didn't disappear but increased. From one day to the next I developed a horrific rash on my face which finally was diagnosed as rosacea type 3. Many dermatologists claimed it was an incurable illness. I was suffering badly from this condition. I looked terrible, my skin hurt and for almost one year no cream or treatment gave me any relief. What made this unbearable and intimidating state even worse was the fact that I didn't attract many paying clients and creating business and working with my few clients felt like hard, joyless, draining work. I was so frustrated.

Then one night I woke up and suddenly all was crystal clear in my head and in my heart: "It's not out there, it's inside of me!" I no longer could drain and compromise my soul. I needed to stop searching on the outside and stop depending on business and medical gurus. I sensed this growing strength that felt nourishing, loving and warm inside. I guess this was the first time that I really saw and embraced myself fully. I had been doing all those apprenticeships for the sake of future success. It was all about the outside world and outside success. How could I miss out consulting the only expert that was capable of showing me the way? How could I miss going inwards and tap into my heart and soul?

The first thing I did the next morning was to make time to create. I've always been a creative person and also offered body wisdom art to my clients but I didn't allow or make the time for being playful myself anymore. I created pieces of way showing and transformative art by using my body as a framework. While letting go of the outcome and opening up to incredibly valuable portals of insight, I started receiving information from my body and soul on such a deep level. Being in some sort of stabilizing flow where nothing needed to, but everything could happen, I discovered a creative compass to my personal truth. This day was the initial step back on a path full of joy, trust and feminine strength. I expanded my experience of getting out of my head and dropping into my heart in many other ways. Using my intelligent mind and also inviting rest, peace and silence felt so expansive to me.

Yet I couldn't grasp exactly what was going on. My focus from needing to achieve and making things become a success shifted to activities that weren't business-related. At least not at first sight. To mention a few examples for my "new" activities and subtle shifts, I started participating in an ongoing intensive intuitive training for my own development and joy. Also I took an in-depth apprenticeship in Human Design to understand my energetic blueprint better. I finally wanted to discover and embrace all my hidden facets and gems. I wanted to know who I really was. I made space for meeting other amazing women and tuning into celebrating Celtic rituals, learning about tantric healing and gathering herbs for healing the body, mind and soul. Moreover, I found my way back into painting and writing and even started participating in a broad range of improv trainings, even on stage. I rediscovered that spending more time in nature for relaxation, meditation or for doing Vision Walks, was an incredibly nourishing and enlightening way to get out of my head and finding all the answers that moved me forward on my aligned path.

At the same time, I weeded out everything that didn't feel aligned and joyful to me. I still remember my business coach's voice, saying that business was not about me but about the way I showed up and that I needed to let my dreams and visions die. I was told to box myself for the sake of success. With my increasing inner awareness and growing inner antennae of what feels right, I stopped participating in this paid business program whose system was a one-size-fits-all approach, ignoring my personality and my soul's desires. Furthermore, I revisited everything that needed to be cleared out in my energetic field. This included doing still more healing work. I let go of imprints from past experiences, bad memories and conditioning that made me repeat my well-known but very exhausting and maybe even destructive, masculine pattern. Of course, I took a closer look at my relationship with my dad and put light on the hidden parts of myself that I finally could integrate. Now I no longer need the validation and appreciation from the outside.

I allowed an expansion from being a striving, successful woman to being a thriving successful and fulfilled woman. With everything I do today, my leading questions are: "Am I feeling joyful?" and "Does this feel aligned?" If the answers are no, I double-check on what to do about it. If it is something that needs to be done, I try to delegate it to someone. And if it is something that's not essential for my life and work, I simply let it go.

Looking back on my amazing path from dropping out of my successful career to finally being a fulfilled and soul-led entrepreneur makes me think of it as an alchemical journey of my soul. In retrospective it feels like an immense expansion or metamorphosis and an integration of my feminine side, while honouring my masculine energies. As soon as I paid attention to my natural cycles of being and doing, of giving and receiving, of withdrawing and showing up, I regained so much strength. The minute I trusted my gut and started developing a strong relationship with my intuition and innate wisdom, no more doctor's appointments were necessary. I activated the healer inside. The pain and the severe skin issues decreased and finally healed completely. I see the body as a magnificent and intelligent messenger and accurate compass towards a fulfilled life. As soon as I let go of the self-made prison of perfectionism and the false narrative around worthiness, I could tap into my beautiful, creative and playful self and access states of flow and pure bliss.

123

Integrating my feminine strengths made my business flourish all by itself. It was as if suddenly everything effortlessly fell into place. People magically showed up and were attracted by the aligned person I had become.

Today my work no longer feels exhausting. I neither need to compare and doubt myself nor do I judge others or compete with them. With confidence and conviction I can say that I am a well-balanced icon in my field and an inspiration for those who also want to embrace, integrate and utilize their true potential.

If you are intrigued by my journey and want to find out how to expand and grow yourself, visit my website at *www.patricialindner.com*. I absolutely love inviting those who are ready to fill this growing void inside themselves through the blissful and transformational metamorphosis of their soul to come play with me.

ABOUT THE AUTHOR
PATRICIA LINDNER

Patricia Lindner is a multi-passionate Soul Alchemist and Creative Instigator.

She inspires and invites accomplished women and men to discover, integrate and utilize their creative and intuitive power, both for their private life and successful career. She believes that life is a canvas and that everyone is able to co-create an extraordinary and fulfilled life beyond outer success.

Also referred to as Travel Guide for the Soul, her holistic anti-coaching approach ensures logic-defying, instant results and revelations. Besides highly customized 1:1 experiences she also hosts international retreats that ensure joy, adventure and transformation on many levels.

Patricia resides in Germany with her husband and two children. When she isn't preparing or hosting transformational experiences for her clients, she is writing, traveling or creating art.

You can connect with Patricia at *www.patricialindner.com*

Facebook : www.facebook.com/patricialindnersoulalchemist
Instagram: www.instagram.com/patricialindnersoulalchemist
LinkedIn: www.linkedin.com/in/patricia-lindner-2857591a4

DR. PIPER GIBSON,
AHND, TND, BCDNM

FROM JEANS TO GENES

For as long as I can remember, I wanted to be a Fashion Designer, and it may have all started when my best friend received fashion plates for her birthday. If you are a child of the '80s, you know what I am talking about here. You mixed and matched tops and bottoms and then used sketch paper and rubbing crayons to make totally awesome outfits. I thought it was the coolest, and I knew then that I wanted to design amazing clothes for people to wear in real life. I took art classes and started entering design competitions in high school. I also designed and created many of my own unique outfits. In college, I worked in retail stores and even took on an internship at Neiman Marcus. I was on my way. I earned a B.S. in Clothing, Textiles, and Fashion Merchandising and went to work for a denim manufacturer right out of college.

I was hired to be a designer, merchandiser, and fit model. Keep in mind that I am not a "model" in any way, I am short, small, and muscular, but they needed an actual human who was a size 5 to try out all the designs. I couldn't wait; I had finally made it to "the industry". I was beyond disappointed when I quickly figured out that it was not glamorous, fun, or exciting. I felt like a quickly deflating balloon and wondered what I had gotten myself into. It was more of a sweatshop atmosphere in a massive warehouse with rooms of sewing machines, giant rolls of fabric, and industrial washers and dryers. I was ordering buttons and zippers and ensuring that the pockets were being sewn on the jeans correctly. Much like the old fashion plates, I used stencils to make prep sheets of what each style would look like. My cubicle was in a giant office that was the color of green hospital scrubs, and the secretary who was across from me had a huge window where she refused to let any sun in. I felt like I worked in a dungeon or at least a big industrial warehouse. I worked with a bunch of older men, and the owner was a tyrant who would rant, rave, and yell at everyone whenever he felt like flying off the handle.

Within the first six months, I knew that this was not for me, and it was quite possibly the worst job I had ever had. I had created this fantastic glamorous scenario in my head and built it up to expect an out-of-this-world experience, and I was miserable. How could I have spent all this time in college learning all these skills and chasing my dreams only to realize that my reality sucked?

I saw my friends working for a non-profit; helping others, and I thought, "That's what I want to do." So after six months in the sweatshop, I left one corporate job for another. I spent the next six years working for the American Red Cross doing public relations, special events, and bookkeeping. Although it was a great job, the American Red Cross got some bad press about how they spent donations, and many of the local chapters took a hit, management changed, and the job took a turn for the worse. It was no longer enjoyable, and I was beginning to feel like maybe the 9 to 5 was not for me.

Since fashion was out and non-profits were struggling, what was I going to do? I started to explore my passions while trying to figure out my next move. Around this time, I became a mom, and I knew then that the corporate gig would not cut it anymore. I struck out on my own, trying everything from Mary Kay to owning an online boutique with my mom and sister. Did I love it? No. Was I out of the 9 to 5? Yes.

Did I feel pulled to do something else? 100%

Little did I know that my life was about to change in a big way, and it was like being hit by a freight train. What happened next would completely change the trajectory of my life and eventually lead me to my passion.

When my oldest son, Whit, was between four and six, he started clearing his throat and sniffing. At that time, we didn't give it a lot of thought and assumed that it was another allergy.

When he turned six, he had such a colossal symptom that we simply could not ignore. We had gone on a family trip to Disneyland and allowed the kids to go hog wild on junk food, snacks, and anything you could think of. The day after we arrived home from the vacation, Whit woke up and started to blink and jerk his neck. We were terrified and had no idea what was going on. He had no control over these movements, and they were so repetitive and aggressive that we were starting to freak out. My husband recorded a video of the whole incident, and off we went to the pediatrician. The doctor looked at him for a few minutes and diagnosed him with a transient neurological tic. We also found out he had an ear infection, and were given antibiotics and told, "Just ignore the tic. He will grow out of it."

It sounded scary, and I was scared! "What is wrong with his brain?" The pediatrician said, "It's probably nothing; he will grow out of it. I would like to see what the neurologist says," and he sent us on our way.

What in God's name is a neurological tic? So my husband and I started reading books and scouring Dr. Google for information on tics while we waited for our neurologist appointment. We found out that tics could last for a short period and that he may experience uncontrollable movements or make vocal sounds like clearing his throat.

After waiting for weeks, I vividly remember sitting in the neurologist's office for the first time, and he said, "Just ignore it; I think your son just needs a good spanking!"

I sat there with my mouth open, looking at my husband, astonished that this was even a suggestion! Symptoms were getting worse, and I remember thinking, *WTF, ignoring it isn't working, how could spanking him help? Is this guy CRAZY??*

His little body was snowballing downhill, and nothing was working. Finally, we were at the neurologist to get to the bottom of his tics and none of this was helpful! We had spent so much time in and out of doctors' offices in the last few months, and they were not my jam. He was only six years old and couldn't control the movement of his body. I was floored and confused, and as I looked from the doctor to my husband, all I could think was, *This is the worst medical advice that we have received so far.*

My maternal intuition told me something was seriously wrong!

At that very moment, I committed to NEVER going back there again. It was clear to me then that the conventional approach had failed us.

Ignoring it was UNACCEPTABLE, and I vowed I would not go down this path any longer.

Over time his tic symptoms worsened and developed into motor tics that included jerking and blinking. It later evolved into chronic throat clearing. We couldn't go to the movies, go out in public or control his movements or the noise he was making. It was heartbreaking, and yet there were no answers in sight.

We didn't have anyone to give us advice or hold our hand, and the response from most of the doctors we saw was, "Just ignore it."

By this point, it was my goal to learn everything I possibly could about tics. I felt like there had to be an answer out there somewhere. Unfortunately, my husband read tons of pub-med studies and nothing on YouTube provided a positive outlook on tics and Tourette's. All the facts and materials at my disposal were screaming at me to ignore what was happening. Yet, I was so sure, deep down in my maternal soul, that there was a lot still going on.

We had already spent a fortune on tests, medicine, supplements, and doctor's consultation fees. We'd been told by several doctors to ignore it, that he would outgrow it; others offered us drugs with scary side effects, and those prescriptions didn't even work. We tried eight different medications that didn't work.

My son's challenge in school was so terrible that I had no choice but to homeschool him. We visited every doctor and specialist around for at least six years without any significant change. I was so frustrated and overwhelmed that I was tempted to pull out my hair.

I often cried in rooms full of other mothers begging for their prayers because I was at my wit's end. I had prayed and spent so many nights screaming into my pillow, asking God to give me answers. I started to believe that that was his destiny and that he had to live with this for the rest of his life. I tried my best as a mother, spending hours, weeks, months, and years carrying out research, looking for answers. I became a mega-researcher as I studied everything from diet to genetics. I started to think outside the box, seeking out options that might help him recover. I read articles, journals, books, magazines, and anything that contained information that might help. I knew what I had to do, and that was to go back to school and relearn everything I thought I knew about health and wellness. If there were not enough info on tic disorders, I would research it, track it, and figure it out myself. I had to take back control and take my son's health into my own hands.

As I continued my studies, one day, a friend called me on the phone and told me about a girl she read about in the newspaper who had similar symptoms to Whit. In addition, she said to me that an alternative allergist had helped that girl. Once I heard this, I grabbed the phone and made an appointment immediately. For the first time, I was hopeful that we had finally met someone who could direct us and set us on the right path.

During our first meeting, the allergist took a glance at him and said, "He is allergic to dairy and gluten. He also has a Candida overgrowth. I can tell by looking at him but let's run some tests."

She tested Whit for food allergies and food sensitivities, which proved she was entirely correct in her diagnosis. Whit was allergic to dairy, wheat, gluten, peanuts, eggs, and soy. These also happen to be the top six inflammatory foods. For the first time, we began to notice improvements in the tics due to the treatments. Although they didn't completely go away, we saw progress. His symptoms also included mood swings, meltdowns, difficulty concentrating and handwriting. The doctor also diagnosed him with sensory processing disorder and recommended that we undergo occupational therapy. Although things had improved significantly, our progress was still not enough, nor was it close to anything I wanted. She later advised that he had an MTHFR (methylenetetrahydrofolate reductase) gene variant. As time went on, I dug deeper and studied even more, trying hard to find the answer I sought. The more we saw her, I had more questions. Finally, she said that I had gone far beyond her scope of practice and suggested I find someone who could help me in genetics.

Before I could even start researching to find an expert, my sister called me and said she had seen someone mention a genetic doctor in Austin, Texas. I was not pumped about the appointment, but I was willing to give it a shot because we had tried everything, and although changing his diet helped somewhat, I knew we were missing a piece of the puzzle.

The doctor advised us to do some nutrigenomic testing, which involves collecting an oral DNA sample from inside his cheeks. Nutrigenomics is the blend of both genetics and nutrition. At the end of our meeting, my husband wondered if all of this was snake oil, how could his genes give us a clue?

However, I was optimistic that this test would hold some of the answers we were looking for. Once we had the results, we had a clear step-by-step plan based on my son's genes – no more shooting in the dark. We knew what we needed to do. Based on his genetics, we were sure that he is susceptible to chronic aggressive inflammation. He was not the best methylator and was reactive to glutamates. We also needed to do some additional nutrient and detoxification support to pull him out of the vortex.

We began to see incredible rapid changes in his health, and I quickly fell in love with genomics. It was a game-changer for us, and I knew that it could be a game-changer for other families going through the same thing.

My passion was born along this crazy journey, and the years of research lit me up in ways I never imagined. We had been in such a dark place with Whit's health, and I spent years feeling frustrated, scared, and overwhelmed. But, although our struggle was intense, we had finally seen the light at the end of the tunnel and what we had overcome was mind-blowing.

I knew that other families needed support; they needed guidance and someone who could hold their hand through the dark times. So many parents are stuck in this conventional box, thinking that there is a pill for every ill and that there is some magical cure that will make it all better overnight. I know I was. Everything that we had been through had shown me that there was a different way: diet, lifestyle, and genes matter.

There was no turning back from the educational journey, and I began taking every class and certification I could find. I needed to arm myself with as much information as possible, and by the time we had seen nutrigenomics, I had already completed the first of many functional health programs. I was now a Certified Functional Diagnostic Nutrition Practitioner®, and I knew nutrigenomics had to be my next certification. I had to get other parents to get this testing done, so I started attending live training classes and soaking up everything I could find on the topic of nutrigenomics and genetics. Not long after that, I became a certified nutrigenomic specialist.

When family, friends, and locals saw the changes that we had experienced, they started coming to me for advice, and that was my sign …

Goodbye corporate world, hello natural health and wellness. I opened Regenerating Health in 2018 and, for the first time, I finally felt passionate and alive in my career. *"How could a child's illness change our lives in so many ways?"* It was vital for me to keep studying because there was still so much I didn't know. I wanted to learn all there was to know about

Holistic Nutrition and Naturopathy, and I went from research mom to Dr. Gibson. I earned two doctorates and also became Board Certified in Natural Medicine. My focus was to help families just like mine whose children were struggling with tic disorders. I wanted to help other moms who felt scared, frustrated, and overwhelmed and give them access to the tools and resources I never had, which I could now provide for them. I would connect the dots for them and show them that even though they were being told to ignore their child's symptoms, there was indeed a connection between symptoms and test results.

I am a scientist at heart, a lover of knowledge and learning. When I have a big burning question to answer, my soul feels alive and I feel passionate about what I am doing. When I look back on my life I was always researching and craved a deeper understanding of most things in life. I think the fashion industry was stifling for me because there were no big burning questions which left me feeling drained and depleted. Jeans provided no outlet for studies and research, it wasn't until my son got sick that I came to the realization that I have a passion for learning, knowledge, and helping others along the way.

If I knew then what I know now, I would have done things differently. However, the path we took was ours to own. It gave us a manual to help us explore a different type of life. My eyes needed to be opened to much more than just tic symptoms; I needed to see his whole body differently. If you want to see changes, you may have to step outside the box to see the big picture. Humans need to feel connected to their bodies, in tune with what is going on. The conventional medical approach focuses on a reductionist health theory, looking at one system or symptom, and never asking "Why?" This conventional approach meant we ended up in a cycle of trial and error and never had any clear answers.

This entire experience has given me the passion, courage, and confidence to step up and live beyond my wildest dreams. I have created a thriving business helping others. I have been featured in several media outlets; I have been featured on podcasts and TV shows. I have made some stellar connections with people in the health and wellness industry, and I would not be where I am today without this struggle.

I went from dreaming of jeans to loving genes. I have to be completely honest here, I still have a toe in the corporate world, but it is on my terms this time. In 2019 my phone rang, and it was GX Sciences, the genetic testing company we used that changed our lives. They were looking for a genomics specialist to educate other providers on genetics and use genomic testing in their practice. You can't just hire a genomic specialist off the street. I could keep working with my clients, but now I would reach many more people with this life-changing testing. I currently work for GX Sciences part time, teaching the world about the power of genomic testing.

I know with 100% certainty that we have the power to create a life beyond our wildest dreams and will continue to pursue that with confidence for the rest of my life.

*If you are a parent who is scared, frustrated, and overwhelmed when it comes to your child's tic disorder, I want you to know that, as a practitioner and a parent, I am confident that tics are not just something that has to do solely with the brain. Tics are similar to the engine warning light on your dash. When something is wrong with your car, the light gives you a warning; it's time to get your vehicle to the shop. In the same vein, tics are the child's body screaming for help. A tic is not the problem; it is a sign that there is a problem. If your child is struggling with a tic and you are looking for a professional hand holder the best place to start is with the Tic Disorders Cheat Sheet and you can grab that on my website: *www.regenerating.health*

ABOUT THE AUTHOR
DR. PIPER GIBSON, AHND, TND, BCDNM

Dr. Piper Gibson, AHND, TND, BCDNM

Regenerating Health

Piper Gibson is a Doctor of Advanced Holistic Nutrition, Traditional Naturopathic Doctor, and is a Board-Certified Doctor of Natural Medicine. Piper helps scared, frustrated, and overwhelmed parents get access to the tools and resources they need so they can get a start to reduce their child's tic disorder symptoms naturally.

She is the founder of Regenerating Health and has been able to help many families all over the world to gain control of their child's neurodevelopmental issues using food, functional lab testing, and natural approaches.

She resides in New Mexico with her husband and two sons. When she isn't working in the health space you can find her relaxing at the lake with her family.

You can connect with Piper at *www.regenerating.health.com*

Facebook : *www.facebook.com/RegeneratingHealth*
Instagram: *www.instagram.com/regeneratinghealth*

RAEWYN GUERRERO

BEING THE CEO OF YOUR HEALTH

"While the beauty is in the butterfly,
growth happens in the cocoon!"
– Jim Kwik

I will always remember the morning I forced myself out of my London flat to get to my Canary Wharf desk job on time. Working in Canary Wharf was my dream when I first arrived in London. But on this frosty Monday in March, it was a little too frosty for someone from the warm and sunny Caribbean Island that had been my home for 22 years.

I was coming from a place where, to avoid violence, women had to get in a car to go anywhere. Roaming freely through the streets of London was not just thrilling, it was liberating!

In 2001, when I was young, and not yet jaded by eight million people all cramming into an overcrowded tube car, it was exciting. I felt alive. Free.

I was part of something bigger. Living in a big city in a first-world country, anything was possible. London was where I would make my mark!

But, by January 2016, the zest for life within that wide-eyed, innocent girl had faded to a faint memory. The novelty of big-city life had lost its shine. By then, the thought of rushing to the tube station was no longer a source of excitement. In fact, the never-ending cold and grey compounded with the thought of another ten-hour day at a desk in a prestigious London Bank now filled me with panic and dread. The knot that was painfully tightening in my bloated belly that icy morning is another memory I can do without.

My sleep the night before had been broken, so waking up that day felt like I was peeling my body out of bed. But this was no different to the 32 Mondays that had gone before. I could not believe I'd been doing this dismal dance for almost a year! Cue the Talking Heads tune "Once in a Lifetime" and David Byrne's infamous and haunting line … "You may ask yourself; how did I get here?"

For ten years before this, I had been so full of life and passion for creating and leading the Wellness Program at the bank. I'd given most of my adult life to it! But now my mother's voice was often the one echoing in my head …

I can just see it in the papers now, **Wellness program manager can't stomach her own medicine.**

The irony hadn't been lost on me. Talk about "imposter syndrome"!

Imagine being a corporate wellness manager with an ever-increasing list of her own symptoms, and a pharmacy in her purse to match. I thought I'd done all the right things. I exercised every day. I ate a strict vegetarian diet. I always chose low-fat products. But somehow, I'd run out of steam. And my mood was prone to dramatic fluctuations. My partner at the time and I were trying to get pregnant, without success. If that wasn't bad enough, my specialists diagnosed me with asthma, anxiety, and depression. Not to mention irritable bowel syndrome (IBS).

As I stood in the communal hallway of my flat, my partner took a photo of my face … That photo was the beginning for me. When I look back on it – the red cheeks, puffy eyes from crying, shoulders drooping in a winter coat, and my aura depleted – I knew I couldn't continue this way. I wasn't free anymore. I was enslaved into a system that was sucking the life out of me.

And I was no longer free in my own body. This was my wake-up call.

Getting my Freedom Back

With a mortgage on a Central London apartment, financial freedom seemed illusive. Working 10 to14-hour days meant that time-freedom had pretty much evaporated, but I was determined to sort things out and turn them around.

Geographical freedom was still in my favour. In the years leading up to this moment, I became a British Citizen, providing me a certain level of flexibility regarding where I could live and work in the world. But if I was going to relocate, it would require a tremendous leap of faith! And it would require me to get my health back and land in an optimal place.

Today, I write to you as the founder of an online wellness business committed to changing the health trajectory of everyone I meet, while overlooking the Arches of Cabo San Lucas, Mexico, where I spend my mornings sitting in the sun drinking collagen mushroom coffee and my days helping burnt-out women uncover the root cause of their symptoms via my laptop, so they can live freely, knowing exactly how to nourish mind, body and soul.

Re-defining Health

Freedom. That word again. The one that drives all of us entrepreneurs. Yes, we want to solve problems, but ultimately our goal is to make the world a better place, while we have fun doing so.

While what I went through came to a head in 2016, the dysfunction had been percolating for years. There were so many signs along the way that despite my best intentions to address them, were largely being looked at through the lens of treating symptoms. Which is why I now love being able to sit down with my clients and look at their entire history. Physical symptoms definitely play a huge part but, believe it or not, the emotional triggers along their life journey are equally relevant, and often don't get the attention they deserve.

You might be thinking, well isn't that what a psychotherapist is for?

Yes, and no.

In my experience, having been through psychotherapy, I have seen that the reopening of wounds repeatedly very seldom leads to healing. Women come to me after seeing therapists for years, and are still not well, are still dealing with the same issues they started off with and, on top of that, they've got physical complaints to add to their list. They're so stuck in their heads that they forget that the chief function of the body is to carry the brain around, according to Thomas Edison. What that means is that the body needs to be in an optimal place if the brain, and subsequently the mind, are to function well.

What is meant by "optimal place"?

That might conjure up images of marathon runners, body builders or supermodels, but this perception of "healthy" is really part of the problem and, in fact, is far removed from what true cellular health is!

What do I mean by "cellular health"?

Cellular health means your body is getting exactly what it needs for every cell, tissue, and organ to function perfectly and in harmony with each other. And I'm sorry if this bursts your bubble but training three hours a day can actually lead to the complete opposite of that.

Over-training puts excessive demand on stress hormones like adrenaline and cortisol. If you use a banking analogy, these hormones produced in the adrenal glands are meant to be used as emergency funds, not like a continuous line of credit. But the way that we live currently, we're under intense pressure to "have it all" – the perfect job, the perfect relationship and, if there's room, the perfect kids. Then, on top of that, we still better look good! This becomes more challenging as the years go by and more responsibilities and obligations are piled upon our plates.

We begin running low on our "adaptive reserves" and enter into an exhaustive phase – like I did. Things start going wrong, but rather than acquiesce to the lifestyle makeover we need, we carry on. Why do we continue to treat our bodies like a vehicle we refuse to service, only taking it to the mechanic (doctor/therapist) to get a tire or two patched up, and then wondering why we aren't running our best or simply break down?

It's easy to see why people don't hit the brakes to re-evaluate whether they are even headed in the right direction. They're bombarded with conflicting information! One minute you should go Keto, the next minute you need to intermittently fast, or you should go vegan. Nutrition has never been a one size fits all! Even though the vegan diet works amazingly for your friend, it may not work for you. It could even make you worse.

Personalised Nutrition in Action

Case in point. My client had a history of Obsessive Compulsive Disorder (OCD) after experiencing trauma in her teens. We started with hypnotherapy, but I soon discovered her history included multiple medications for various other ailments including bloating and pain. When I inquired about nutrition, she said, "Well I gave up meat and decided to go vegan."

I asked, "And how do you feel since going vegan?"

"Horrendous. I'm constantly bloated and in pain."

"Oh no. What makes you feel better?"

"When I eat fish and vegetables."

"Marvellous. Can you go back to eating like that?"

"But I thought going vegan was healthy!"

"Clearly not for you," I said, and we went on, through Functional Labs, to discover the right diet for her.

We embarked on an investigative journey to uncover exactly what would work best for her body. We examined gut health and food sensitivities. One of the reasons I fell in love with Functional Medicine was because it put an end to the cycle of trial and error that I, like my clients, was stuck in. There was no more, "Maybe you should try this" or "Maybe you should try that."

The lab work allows us to zero straight into what's going on in the body on various levels. By having that clarity and precision, we're no longer wasting time wondering what new fad you should try, and your headspace is free to help solve the real problem. With the right lab work, you finally have tangible evidence that you can work with to help you re-invent your lifestyle.

The right information helps to form a roadmap that is uniquely yours. When you start working on yourself in this way, looking at Diet, Rest, Exercise, Stress Reduction and using Supplements (DRESS) strategically, huge shifts in energy can happen very quickly. These breakthroughs extend into all other areas of your life. You suddenly have the time to think about what you really want, you begin to prioritize your heart's desires, the things that light you up!

How often do you devote to thinking, *What are the things I actually love to do and how often am I doing them?*

If Not Now, When

I remember vividly sitting down with a friend in Spitalfields Market in London after coming back from the Institute for Functional Medicine Conference in Miami in June 2018. I told my friend how much I love being by the ocean and around like-minded people like the ones I'd connected with at the conference. She looked at me and said, "Then why don't you find a way to make the move?"

I shot her a look of incredulity.

"What, leave London?"

She continued matter-of-factly, "Yeah, if you're happier in America by the ocean, I'm sure you can figure out how to make it happen."

The spark had been ignited. Instead of sitting around whingeing in the all-too-common British fashion, I was catapulted into action. That conversation hit me with the realisation that my life was flying past me, and I was just sitting there wishing it away when I could be channelling that energy into living with intention and living by design.

Do you ever do this? Do you talk yourself out of going for what you want?

Oh, don't be silly. I could never do that.

Or you produce a million and two reasons why now is not the time for you to make that dream a reality ... or why you cannot do what you really want – just yet. In hindsight, I see that it was no coincidence that on the eve of my launch event for Well Works, I got a call from my mother telling me that she had stage one endometrial cancer.

I was devastated for her and shaken to my core with the profound realization that women, in particular, may live all their lives working hard, caring for their loved ones, and delaying their dreams until they retire. But, by then, their bodies may be worn out and diseased – and suddenly, there's no time for all the things they wished they'd done.

My intention is for this book to be your wake-up call! Let it be the antidote to that negative voice in your head telling you what you cannot do. It is time. Do not wait another second. Are you ready to start living, rather than just being caught in the business of living?

What small action can you take to get you started realising your dream today?

Will you commit to understanding the ins and outs of your body and your brain?

Work Smarter Not Harder – Marry Your Motivations with Your Metabolism

When I began my business, I needed to know this information if I was going to succeed. Embarking on a dream that one is so enthusiastic about can have its downsides. You may forget to tend to your physical needs and that is something everyone considering a career change must be mindful of. If you feel that your current role has been sucking the life out of you, how much of that is actually about the way you function and think?

While I am grateful that I burnt out in my corporate job, as it was the catalyst to start my own business, I saw very quickly how easy it would be to burn out working for myself! Poor boundaries had always been an issue for me, and they were glaringly obvious in my own business. I had such a strong drive to put other people's needs ahead of my own. I learned that from my West Indian mother. I often failed to draw the line on my own downtime and self-care.

There were days when I would work 15 hours solidly, replying to client's questions over texts on evenings and weekends. I did that because I had to prove to myself that I could do this. And I needed to give these clients a type of care they had never received from other practitioners – someone who listens to them and responds. In the UK, you never have contact with your doctor or your therapist outside of your scheduled appointment time. Doctors see you for a maximum of 15 minutes; with therapists, you usually get, "That's all we have time for today" at 55 minutes.

I hated that. I used to feel like I was just starting to open up at 55 minutes and then it was time to stop. So, I set out to give my clients an experience that I would have wanted. However, I did not realize how all-consuming it would become when you have 20 clients! It meant that you

145

could never predict if Saturday night or Sunday morning would be incident free. This meant that my downtime was often interrupted.

This was one of my first epiphanies to preventing burn-out in my new life. Yes, I was doing what I loved professionally, but what about the other things I needed to sustain my joy and energy? What was I doing to recover? When was I having fun?

The beauty of working for yourself is that you get a chance to reflect, reassess, and redirect! I put the brakes on and took a deep, long, hard look at the way things were going. I realized I needed help! I invested in a year-long mastermind program that offered peer support plus one-on-one mentorship that absolutely changed my life. I found out that I was not alone in wanting to be all things to all people! This is a common issue that coaches and therapists face.

JP Morgan said: *"I can do the work of a year in 9 months but not in 12."*

If you want to perform at an elevated level, you need periods of recovery. The day off, the evenings and weekends off, even a few weeks off, all help you last longer and better!

I once listened to an interview with Tal Ben-Shahar, the Harvard University Positive Psychology guru, who reminded me to look at the Formula 1 race car driver. He worries that if he takes a pit stop, others will overtake him. The reality is that if he keeps going, he is either going to burn out his tyres, or he'll run out of fuel.

If you want to perform and be at your happiest and healthiest, you need to take pit stops and schedule recovery times.

I became good at scheduling recovery because I didn't want to fail at this new life that I was now 100% responsible for creating. Think about it like this; if you go to the gym and lift heavy weights, continuously increasing your load all in the same day, you will end up injured.

Why? Because you have not had enough downtime or recovery to give your muscles time to rest and then grow. Exercise is important but rest is what allows the muscles to grow!

Think of your body like a rubber band. If you're stretching continuously, you'll lose elasticity and you'll break. But if you allow that rubber band to spring back into shape regularly by getting good-quality sleep, the right kind of foods, exercise and supplements, that rubber band is going to retain elasticity.

It is great to make sure you're eating right for you, you're getting great sleep, and you're scheduling downtime and fun time to recharge your energy. However, you also need to be laser focused on where you direct that energy so that it's not wasted, and it actually turns into something productive.

What I got most out of the mastermind program was that in order to stay balanced, I needed a system; one that I could turn on at the start of a working day and turn off in the evenings and weekends. One where clients could reach me only during working hours, rather than receiving random texts on my phone that jerked me out of my recharge time and back into the office.

You will need a similar program when you decide to venture out on your own so you can draw the line, protect your downtime, and continue to love your business as you grow.

Even with all its peaks and valleys, this journey has been nothing short of incredible. While I do not wish the dark days of my own physical health struggle on anyone, they were pivotal in the birthing of this new reality. Now I can get to activate fellow freedom seekers transform their entire way of being – mind, body, and spirit – so they can create a life beyond their dreams, while I continue to live in places that I'd only ever dreamed of!

Someone from my old banking life recently reached out to me to say that she could not believe how I had reinvented myself in the four years since I left my corporate job. I thought about her words but decided that 'reinvented' was not right, I'd simply grown into the person I'd always wanted to be.

ABOUT THE AUTHOR
RAEWYN GUERRERO

Raewyn Guerrero is the Gutsy Executive Coach, Speaker, and Founder of Well Works, an online Functional Medicine Practice and Corporate Wellness Consultancy, committed to helping high-performing women eliminate the guesswork around your stress, so that you can fine-tune your biochemistry and become the CEO of not only your health, but your Life. By offering a personalised roadmap for how to eat, think, sleep and move through the insights gained from Functional Labs, she's set to change the face of healthcare and create a Well World. After years of chasing symptoms to address her Anxiety and IBS, she founded Well Works – her online Functional Medicine Practice and Corporate Wellness Consultancy – with a team of practitioners who share her vision of **self-care as healthcare**. While leading Wellness at Barclays PLC between 2011–2016, Raewyn was a member of the UK All Party Parliamentary Group for Mindfulness in the Workplace. She's been featured in the **Huffington Post, the CW Network,** and on numerous podcasts discussing a Nutrition and Psychology approach for **Sleep, Panic Attacks and Anti-Aging.**

Facebook: www.facebook.com/groups/wellworksworld
LinkedIn: www.linkedin.com/in/raewynwellworks
Instagram: https://www.instagram.com/gutsyexecutivecoach

RAI HYDE

THE BLACK SHEEP WHO BECAME THE ALPHA WOLF

I sat across the table from a man who was coming down off meth, his eyes darting all around the room. My job as a triage specialist was to complete his admission to the mental hospital. Yet, I couldn't do that while he was still seeing monsters climbing the walls and hearing a cacophony of buzzing from deep within his own head. So I sat with him and I waited.

This was the third time I had seen this man. After recognizing him, I spoke with my supervisor, assuming that she would see the pattern as an indication that what we were doing for him wasn't working and it was time to do something different. Instead, she said, "You know what to do," and told me to put him through the same fucking protocol.

Stunned and feeling a strong battle waging between the outside world and my inner world, I watched this man from across the intake room table. And I waited … dreading the decision I would have to make once he was finally able to be admitted.

As a young girl, I was fascinated with the world of magic and nature. Even so much to the point where I would sneakily buy books on paganism and world mythology and hide them from my parents.

I wasn't sure if I believed that the specific color of a candle would be a deciding factor in whether or not a spell would work. I didn't quite buy that in order for you to manifest the reality you wanted, you absolutely *had to* have moon-washed mugwort, lamb's cress, and mayweed. But while I explored magic with interest and could never see myself in any of the religions I read about, I knew for sure that I didn't believe in everything that my family believed in.

From a young age, I knew I didn't believe Jesus was real. I didn't believe that people who weren't Christian were bad and would automatically go to hell. I didn't believe that it was wrong to show someone you love them before a church decided that you could.

Despite trying desperately to make my dad proud by reading the Bible, I knew I didn't believe in it. Nor did I believe that the all-powerful God had a human son. In fact, this went against everything that I knew in my heart and my soul to be true.

As I got older, everything I learned about biology, chemistry, evolution, astrophysics, and more confirmed my beliefs that Christianity was yet another story made up by humans – and it was far smaller than the truth.

Growing up, I was the black sheep of the family. I dressed in ways that my family didn't understand. I was interested in things that they didn't think were right for a young girl. While I wanted to play with K'Nex and go ride my dirt bike, my mother insisted on buying me Barbies and forcing me into becoming a model, even to the point of signing me with Wilhelmina modeling agency.

Because there was no one in my family I felt connected to, I didn't have anyone to help me deal with everything that I was going through with my mother. My mother was an angry, overly competitive woman who worked in a violent and extremely male-dominated field.

As a detective in the gangs unit, my mother didn't know when to turn off her authoritarianism. She brought her cop demeanor, her strictness, her aggression and the violence of her job home with her. And she took it out on the only people who were safe to do so: me and my father.

In response, my father decided not to be home as much as possible. Looking back, I see that it was a subconscious decision; a way for him to avoid the pain and conflict that my mother inflicted in whatever 500 square foot area she occupied. But back then, I just felt alone.

Like my mom, my dad was a cop. He took every opportunity to work overtime – security for movie shoots, Charger games, DUI checkpoints, absolutely anything he could do to be where he felt like he was being of use, helping people, and protecting people – something he couldn't do at home.

On top of that, he ran his own tree-trimming business. So on the two or three days that he did have off from being a cop, he was either working overtime or trimming trees around San Diego County.

Sometimes, if I was lucky, one of those days would fall on a weekend and I would get to go with him. I'm pretty sure I learned how to stack wood before I learned how to tie my shoes. So, from an early age, I learned how to channel my anger, my frustration, and my sadness into work.

Soon after I turned 14, I started making plans to emancipate myself – and I knew that meant I needed money.

I started tutoring kids in math. I beefed up my résumé by volunteering at the local library teaching Spanish-speaking students how to read and write in English. I got my certification as a soccer referee so that, when I wasn't playing in games, I was officiating them.

I stashed away the money my mom gave me to buy lunch at school. Rather than eating, I would save $5 a day in a little pouch shaped like a red M&M.

At 16, I hit my breaking point. I was washing dishes with my mother and I asked her something that, still to this day, I cannot remember. It was so mundane, so simple; just another volley of the conversation back to her. But she snapped.

Apparently, what I said was questioning her authority, or calling her weak or insecure. I'm still not sure. But she lunged at me and I knew, based on so many instances just like this from the past 14 years of my life, that I was in danger.

If I didn't want yet another concussion or more Tabasco sauce forcibly poured down my throat while having the breath choked out of me by her unusually strong grip, I had to run.

And I did.

I ran to my room, my mind laser-focused on one thing: my keys. I knew if I could grab my keys and get out of that house, I could come back when she was at work, get what I needed, and leave for good – on my terms.

I raced to my room. I could feel her right behind me, breathing down my neck. She faltered a bit when I slammed my bedroom door in her face. I found the front pocket of my backpack and got my hand around my little ring of two house keys. I spun around to see her blocking the door. She was seeing red – and I was seeing my only way out. I juked around her and I *flew* out of the front door, barefoot, wearing pajama pants and a tank top.

My heart was pounding in my ears. My breath went only as deep as my heart. I ran all the way down our street, across the gravel, across the soccer field of the elementary school, across the playground, down another street, and another, and another, and another.

At some point I stopped, collapsed onto a curb, and sat – heaving and crying at the same time. I don't know how long I was gone or where I was. All I knew was that she wouldn't find me, and that was good enough.

Three days later, I still hadn't been back in the house and that was the final straw for my father. He realized he had to choose between his child and the woman he married. While he grappled with his decision, we sat in his car in the driveway and I consoled him. I supported my father through that difficult decision. However, it would be years before I got any support, or even got anyone to listen, about what I went through.

A week later, we were living at a campground. I made the decision not to go back for my senior year of high school. Instead, I dropped out.

Now that my dad was with me, I wouldn't have to legally emancipate myself, but I would still have to do everything else required.

I lied about my age on job applications. I took on more tutoring work. And I enrolled in every single community college in a 70-mile radius in order to accumulate the credits I would need to earn my high school diploma.

I was 16 at the beginning of September 2006, officially a high school dropout. By the end of October 2006, I was a high school graduate. I had earned enough credits in Fast Track college courses to finish an entire year's worth of high school in eight weeks.

By this time, my father's brother – my uncle – found out what happened and where we were living – and he wasn't going to stand for it. This was the first time I felt like someone in my family saw me and understood what I was going through.

He and his husband talked and they decided that we were going to move in with them. They extended the invitation to my dad who passed it on to me, and I was overjoyed. I loved my uncle and I admired him so much; but because of my mother's irrational homophobia, she hadn't let me see him since I was about eight years old.

A short while later, my dad and I each had a room at my uncles' three-bedroom, two-bathroom house in San Diego.

Now, with a roof over my head, my plan was in full force. Only now it also involved college applications. I turned 17 in January 2007 and I kept manipulating the community college system to get as many credits as I could.

After I was accepted into five colleges, I chose Santa Clara University where I was able to transfer a number of my credits and start as a sophomore in September 2007.

I was the most regimented first-year college student SCU had ever seen. While my friends were partying at night and staying up late, I was consistently going to bed at 9:30 or 10 o'clock, waking up at 6:30, going to school, and working in between classes.

By the end of my first month at Santa Clara University, I had five jobs on campus, as well as freelance writing online. True to my history, I passed every single course with an A and I was upset if I didn't have a plus at the end of that grade.

I felt free and in my own element; but I still didn't belong. My family on my dad's side still didn't fully know or understand what happened. On my mom's side, nobody ever reached out to me to ask what happened, why I hadn't spoken to my mother in over a year, or why my father and I were now living with his gay brother.

I still felt alone, but I had my work. I had work to do on campus; I had work to do online; and I had my coursework earning a Bachelor of Science degree in Psychology.

I have a theory about those of us who choose the mental health world. I think we do so because we have some healing that still needs to take place. We can understand the people who are receiving the treatment because we've been there, too.

We may not have gotten help, but we've been depressed, anxious, paranoid, afraid, and we can understand them. Because we wanted help so badly when we were in those dark places, we feel like it's our responsibility to help them from our place of empathy and understanding.

So I furthered my plan, doubling-down on the world of psychological torment that I knew so well. Because I knew the law enforcement world so well from being the child of a cop and a gangs detective, and also because I understood depression, anxiety, post-traumatic stress disorder, and personality disorders, I chose to become a counselor in the prison system.

Toward the end of my first year at Santa Clara University, I thought I had found my people, my pack. I had a best friend who many people thought was my sister. And I had a boyfriend who shared the same interest and drive in academics that I did. We also both had a love for travel and foreign languages.

While I thought I had found my home in this small group, one night, I let my guard down and let my desire for belonging stifle my inner voice of knowing and intuition.

I was hanging out with a group of friends and my boyfriend's suitemates; we were all watching a movie, but most people had one eye on the TV and the other eye on their laptops or their cell phones. I had started to relax my set bedtime for the sake of social connection by this time and, while my friends went off and did other things, I stayed to finish the movie.

One of my boyfriend's suitemates stayed, too. After a few minutes, it was just us, but I didn't realize it until it was too late.

Just thinking back to that night as I write this makes my head ring with the pain of my head hitting the corner of a wooden, college-issue dresser. My eyes blur with the stinging tears that came with getting cracked across the face with a strong backhand. My voice gets raspy just thinking back to how much I screamed only to have my face pushed into a pillow where I couldn't breathe.

When he was done, he let me go and said – just as I had heard so many times from my mother – "Don't bother telling anybody. Nobody will believe you." With blood running down my legs, I pulled my pants back up and somehow stumbled out of the suite, my vision impaired by tears and a concussion.

I found myself in the stairwell of our dorm building. I don't know how long I was there crying and clawing at my wrists trying to open my veins just so I could end it on my terms.

A few people walked by me as I lay there on the concrete landing. I can only assume that they were rolling their eyes at the overly dramatic freshman who was probably crying over her final exams.

Eventually one of those people was my boyfriend. Just like how, to this day, I still can't bring myself to say the R word out loud, I couldn't say anything. I couldn't tell him what happened. The words just got choked up in my throat and came out as wails and more tears.

I couldn't speak for days. The next morning, he walked with me to the dining hall. We got our breakfast as usual, but I couldn't chew. My jaw was so sore and swollen that I just mashed a few mouthfuls of eggs against the top of my mouth, swallowed, and gave up.

That was the start of the growing distance between us. A few months later, we broke up, but stayed friends.

Eventually, I got the courage to tell him what happened. He didn't believe me and said he figured I cheated on him. I told my best friend what happened, and she said in response, "Why didn't you fight him off?" Our conversation ended there and never resumed.

After a few months, I started getting death threats from my attacker. Although the campus housing office told me I wasn't allowed to break my housing contract, I decided I wasn't going to live there anymore. Eighteen years old and working only online because I could no longer hold down a job on campus – or anywhere that required me to be at a certain place at a certain time, for that matter – I found myself a room to rent off campus.

Somehow I managed to graduate from Santa Clara University after three years with honors, a year ahead of all of my friends. I moved back to San Diego and enrolled in a graduate program at Brandman University studying Marriage & Family Therapy and Professional Clinical Counseling.

All the while, I was freelancing to pay my way. I had odd jobs – a flower delivery girl, a babysitter, even a telephone-actor for a company that taught professionals how to administer personality tests and psychological evaluations – but none stuck.

Writing was my saving grace. It allowed me to earn an income, working from my apartment, where I felt safe, doing something that I had always known how to do. It was in my DNA; it was in my heart; it was coded onto my soul. It was my lifeline that allowed me the space and flexibility to heal without being forced to walk around in everyone else's world – a world that had grown foreign to me.

Two years after meeting the man who would eventually become my husband, I moved to Texas with him.

I started my second graduate program, this time getting a Master's degree in Criminology. After completing my degree, working at a drug rehab facility, a community counseling center, and now a mental hospital, I thought I had made it after all.

This is what I had been working toward, right? Ever since I left my mother's house and voluntarily dropped out of high school.

But now, as I sat across from this man coming down off meth and watched reality gradually sink into him, I heard my supervisor's words play over and over again in my head: *You know what to do.*

I told myself, *Yes, I do.*

I couldn't bring myself to put this man – who the system obviously wasn't helping – through another treatment protocol of the same ol' bullshit.

So I quit.

My supervisor was livid. But I didn't care. I trusted my gut instinct – something that had been growing inside me over all of these years and all of these challenges; something I would come to realize was my connection to the Universe. It seemed to grow stronger with each passing year, like a voice speaking from deep within my body.

On this day, it shouted with loving, but strong, confident direction: "You don't belong here! You can't help from in here! Get out!"

Anytime I feel the pull to make a seemingly audacious decision, I would hear the voice. "Yes." "No." "Hell, yes!" "Fuck, no!" That voice has never steered me wrong – not once.

Now, after freelancing and being my own independent income-generator for more than 15 years, I know that it's that voice that I was looking for all along. It was my connection to something far greater than myself, my family, or their religion.

While I may have been the black sheep of my family, and my college social circle, and the mental health world, I was never a black sheep to the Universe. I was exactly who I needed to be: an alpha. Someone who wouldn't accept anything forced upon her without a fight. Someone who would pave her own way, create her own path, and walk it standing tall and confident in her ability to provide for herself based on her connection to the Universe.

Since leaving the mental health world, I've grown my freelance writing business into a content marketing agency. Today, we serve more than 30 clients at a time and have more than 20 creatives – including my wonderful husband – on our team.

As I grew my agency, I naturally fell into a mentoring relationship with the ambitious writers and designers on my team.

Now, while I continue to run Cornell Content Marketing, my heart and soul are focused on mentoring self-employed entrepreneurs who, like me, have felt out of place their entire lives. Together, we identify the black sheep side of their identities and honor them by building businesses and lifestyles that allow them to become the alphas of their own lives.

I'm fortunate to be able to live among my own self-made pack of alphas now. True to my own personal history, we're breaking all the rules together. While nature says that there can only be one alpha, we say no. Sure, we go off and run our businesses and our lives independently from one another; but we always have a place to come back to where all of us are respected and revered as alphas in our own right – and we fortify each other to be bigger, better, and stronger than ever before.

ABOUT THE AUTHOR
RAI HYDE

Rai Hyde Cornell is the CEO and Senior Copywriter at Cornell Content Marketing and Business Mentor and Coach at Chiron Consulting.

As a mentor and coach at Chiron Consulting, she works with freelancers and self-employed entrepreneurs to help them dramatically increase their incomes and their quality of life as independent income generators. At Cornell Content Marketing, Rai teaches entrepreneurs and business owners how to use content to build powerful, lasting relationships with customers.

Over her 15+ years in online marketing and writing, Rai has worked in hundreds of businesses, helping them grow and achieve their goals. Though she no longer works in the mental health field, her deep understanding of human behavior, emotion, and decision-making is honored in everything she teaches and creates for her clients.

If you're interested in mentoring with Rai or joining her pack of self-made alphas, visit *www.chironconsulting.us* to learn more about Rai's workshops, courses, group mastermind, and one-on-one mentoring programs.

Facebook Page: *www.facebook.com/chironconsultingus*
Instagram: *www.instagram.com/chironconsulting*
LinkedIn: *www.linkedin.com/in/raicornell*

REBECCA DOBBINS

CHASING YOUR BLISS

As I look back on my career, it is clear to me that I have always had an entrepreneurial spirit. While I never intended to walk away from my full-time "corporate" life – "corporate" being a word I will define shortly – it eventually happened. And I couldn't be happier for it.

Primarily, I worked in the corporate sector, but I also tried my hand at some less permanent, smaller business projects over the years. These entrepreneurial ventures were far more of a side hustle than a full-time gig, and I naturally found myself with thumbs in so many pies that I couldn't quite find the time to commit to my smaller ventures. Being interested in so many things may lead to great small talk, but it certainly made it more difficult to sit down and commit to one career path. In fact, it's still difficult.

Throughout the past 15 years, I have worked as an event planner, a ski instructor, a volunteer, a humanitarian, a small business owner several times over, a life coach, an author and, most recently, and soon to be, fingers crossed, an Airbnb owner. Some of these "titles" were occupations, some were short-term projects, and some were far more long-lasting and lucrative than others. Still, each played a major role in shaping the next step of my career journey and giving me the courage to become a corporate dropout. Despite my opinions and experiences, don't expect me to slam the corporate world and those who partake in it. Some people thrive in those settings as I did for many years. But upon hearing this you may find yourself wondering, then "Why did she ever walk away?"

To me, a "corporate dropout" doesn't mean someone that gave up or someone who failed, it means someone who has decided to look at

164

unconventional work opportunities as a way of finding something that makes them truly happy. We may all be familiar with the typical 9 to 5 desk job, which comes with beloved benefits like medical and dental care, a retirement plan and two weeks' vacation in return for potentially punching a clock and sitting in a cubicle. Within the 9 to 5, you will simply find yourself a number among many in a corporate machine. It has its pros and cons, and it's something that some people love and some find unfulfilling. In contrast, the goal of a less traditional position could be less about traditional business models and more about living your life on terms that make you happy. Taking a more unconventional route doesn't automatically mean you have to open your own business and work for yourself. At the beginning of my career, I worked as an event planner and ski instructor – I loved both jobs and I plan to retire as a ski instructor – but I was working for someone else. In fact, the ski resort I was working for could be defined as a massive corporation. However, my daily tasks and life were not defined by the traditional 9 to 5 and therefore, in the conventional sense, it wasn't a corporate job.

When I worked for an event planning firm in New York, I was always on the go. For example, this ranged from running errands, such as picking up linens, cakes and decor for weddings from local vendors to designing centrepieces for tables and matching stationery for invites, seating cards and thank yous – not to mention coordinating all the logistics on the day of the events. The event company worked with clients to design any tailor-made event they required. In essence, the world was our oyster when it came to creativity! The hours were horrendous, including weekends and holidays, and if anything was not perfect, the clients could be very challenging and understandably so. They were paying a lot of money to have things done a certain way, so managing expectations was also an essential (but tricky) part of the job. Wouldn't you expect an event that cost thousands, hundreds of thousands or even a million dollars, to be perfect? Talk about pressure. It was a great job for a time and I truly enjoyed it, but it was a mere step on my path to self-discovery. Eventually I had to move on to find what kind of employment would make me truly happy.

As a ski instructor, my office was the outdoors, the mountains. I was outside every day, and my job was teaching and exercising with others, with no one to look over my shoulder or micromanage me. I worked alone with my clients who were typically between the ages of three and six which, despite being difficult for some, was an age group I loved to work with. However, I wasn't alone all the time. There was some collaboration between instructors as we shared ideas on how to improve our clients' skills at the daily morning meetings. The best perk of the job was free skiing whenever I wasn't working. I can truly say that not one day was ever the same as the one before and adventure was the name of the game. Nonetheless, as I was not self-employed, I had to follow company rules. We were required to wear uniforms, we had to please the parents, and work was relentless during holiday times, which made seeing my own family during the holidays almost impossible. The job may have had more pros than cons to it but after two seasons of work and graduate school in Europe just over the horizon, my time on the slopes was due to end in the search for something more.

My most substantial career to date, or "corporate" job, has been serving as a humanitarian worker for various international organisations worldwide. For the past 12 years, I have worked with numerous United Nations (UN) agencies and peace operations, as well as non-governmental organizations (NGOs) such as the Nobel Peace Prize Laureate, Doctors Without Borders, helping individuals affected by conflict, natural disasters, and medical crises. My work spanned multiple continents in countries like Iraq, Sudan, South Sudan, Sierra Leone, the Central African Republic, and the Democratic Republic of Congo. I enjoyed my work immensely and loved meeting people from all walks of life, especially my host country colleagues. It was a dream to be paid to work abroad, meet interesting people, learn about cultures first-hand and hopefully make a slight difference in the world. But, with any corporate job, it had its drawbacks. I was away from my friends and family and wasn't always able to go home for the holidays. My life became very unsteady and I easily became ill, often from contact with different infectious diseases. It was part of the job, but it certainly took its toll. Furthermore, as UN workers, we didn't get to choose which country we served so it was an endless rat race of applying for multiple positions, never knowing what we would be offered and where we would be moving to.

In 2015, between missions abroad, I decided to open a brick-and-mortar wellness business in Lugano, Switzerland, the country I called home while on a break from working in the field. I had a few months off and saw a need for a beauty café where women could enjoy spa-like services with American-style customer service. I had a vision that the services would be at a fraction of the cost and time than at a traditional Swiss spa and would come with a stunning view of Lake Lugano. It became more of a gathering place with a lively atmosphere where clients could book group appointments, parties, yoga events and enjoy Aperitivo's with their services or attend pop-up shop events. I loved the idea – it was a perfect outlet for my boredom during my time off, and I grew excited at the prospect of opening a business I could eventually run remotely. At the time I probably should have paid more attention to the difficulties that come with opening a remotely managed business, but with only a few months to open before returning to my full-time job in a war zone, it was now or never. It might sound obvious, but I was caught up in the thrill of the experience too much to worry about those things at first. I became hooked on everything that came with running the shop. From designing to marketing, managing staff and partnering with local vendors, creating holiday events and providing good customer service, it was a hell of an experience that I truly loved. But a small start-up requires funds to reinvest in the first few years to continue growing, and another UN mission soon presented itself. While I was back in the field, I managed my staff and business remotely and I was only able to check-in personally every four weeks during my rest and recovery holiday. This meant that the time I was meant to be resting and spending with my loved ones was soon spent running a business and being just as busy and as stressed as when I was at work. But at the time I didn't care – I simply loved the thrill of having my own business running in the background of my UN career. This continued for three and a half years, but then the space we were renting required renovation, so it was time for us to find a new space. After reviewing start-up costs for a new location, rent and paying salaries in Switzerland, my partner and I decided that, although we were in the green on a monthly basis and starting to recoup our initial investment, the overall costs, both financially and personally, weren't worth it to "start over". The pros simply didn't outweigh the cons, in this case. So I went back to only having one job, my UN work, for a time.

After the thrill of running the business, the negatives of my humanitarian career began to take their toll. I felt that my time with the UN was coming to its natural end after an inward shift in focus. I had enjoyed working as an entrepreneur and my mind started to drift towards doing it again. Although each of my vastly different work experiences were unique, fun, and entertaining in their own right, I was still reporting to others, which, simply put, wasn't allowing me the freedom and happiness I knew I could find elsewhere. Working for myself would give me this and I would be able to utilise my creative side more, which was also incredibly important to me. Leaving humanitarian work felt like such a big leap to take and I certainly had many reservations about resigning from my fixed-term post, but I knew that I wasn't necessarily closing the door on this career forever, just for the time being. I'm not sure if there was one "last straw" that led to me resigning, or more an accumulation of events over time, but continuously moving from conflict zone to conflict zone started to make me feel that I was sacrificing parts of myself and comprising other areas of my life in order to keep up. And that could only last for so long.

It was difficult to step back and say goodbye to humanitarian work, even if only for the time being. It had been my dream job despite the challenges, but I knew it was necessary for me to find a solution to the toll that a non-existent work-life balance was having on me. It was the same position I had been in before in some ways – I hadn't left the corporate world because it was horrible or because I hated it. I left because I knew there were different, and potentially better, opportunities for me elsewhere, and I was willing to take the risk to bet on myself and find them. So, if you find yourself faced with such a difficult decision, do as I did and try not to focus on everything you're leaving behind, but focus on what you stand to gain from trying something new. Just because you're saying goodbye for now doesn't mean you're saying goodbye forever. There's no reason you can't return to your previous career path if you realise eventually that it was the right path for you. Nothing is final.

168

So, following my humanitarian work, I shifted focus from emergency preparedness, coordination and civilian protection with large international organisations to a more direct people-centred approach. This allowed me, as a life coach, to help others transition and find their life's purpose, passion and direction. I think it's important to restate that I'm not sure I will ever commit to one career path for the rest of my life, but that's okay. There is a joy in knowing that I could potentially go back to emergency humanitarian work if I ever wanted to. Although I am currently focused on building my own business and pursuing many creative avenues, I haven't fully closed that door behind me.

At the time of writing this I am at the start of my second and third entrepreneurial ventures. I became a life coach a year ago, coaching clients, partaking in motivational speaking engagements, and occasionally guest lecturing at high schools and universities. I hope to develop a masterclass course or training soon that is focused on helping people discover what I know to be true, that it's possible to achieve a work-life balance and financial independence. Additionally, I enjoy collaborating with other entrepreneurs to create and identify new business and investment opportunities, have authored some chapters in best-selling books, and recently started looking in property to open and run my first rental property. If success is measured by monthly income, then I haven't "made it" yet. However, every day I can do anything and everything I want when I want, which is how I am judging success in my life right now. And, if I'm being honest, I feel pretty damn successful as a result.

Working for anyone other than yourself may be easier when it comes to things like financial security, a reliable pay cheque, retirement funds, medical care but it also comes with its own unique set of challenges. A corporate job is usually controlled by bosses, deadlines, output, attitudes of colleagues etc., which directly affects your outcome and happiness. This varies based on who you work with and for. It is a fact of life that we all need money to live, but if you could make a living and support yourself financially without working for anyone but yourself, why would you not leap at that chance? You can control your work hours, daily schedules and tasks, goals, collaborations, creativity, earnings, vacation time and so forth. As with all decisions in life, there are both positive and negative aspects. I think the question is, "What do you prioritise?" Status? A reliable pay cheque? Independence? If you are self-motivated, you can curate your own life on your terms, which is much more rewarding and will ideally help you achieve whatever dreams you have. And if you're not quite there yet, perhaps it's something to think about.

I think everyone needs to define what happiness and success means to them. Maybe that means walking away from a desk job that takes away a little more than what it gives. If that's the case, it's important to know that we're not alone. It's a slow process to figuring out what makes us happy and what our dreams really are. But sometimes even just taking the time to examine our options can help us decide what we want our future to hold, and that can often come in the form of simply testing the waters. It's important we begin by simply defining what motivates us. It might take work but nobody creates a million-dollar business overnight, or even finds happiness in whatever form it exists to them. If you're looking for a change of pace, perhaps consider starting with smaller-scale projects here and there, experimenting with different ventures and the effect they have on the rest of your life before jumping wholeheartedly into one new source of income. Passive income streams, money that can be earned from different sources without too much ongoing effort and minimal maintenance, can be a great way to dip your toe in and they're also far less of a risk. Examples are rental income, writing an e-book, creating online courses and trainings, buying dividend stocks etc…Simply trusting your creativity and utilising your drive is a great place to start, and for many entrepreneurs, it is more about the journey and experiences than the "success" or financial profits. Ultimately, we all define success differently.

I am only at the beginning of my third self-employed journey now, and by no means would I consider myself a "successful CEO", but I am happier than I have been in a long time. Right now that's enough for me and maybe, one day, it could be for you too.

I hope this inspires you if you want to leave your corporate job but have found you are afraid of starting out on your own. I encourage you to follow your dreams even if you may struggle to get going or feel scared of potential consequences. It is entirely possible to earn money doing what you were born to do when you become brave enough to step outside of the box of everything you know. So, give it a go and see what happens. It might just be the best thing you do.

ABOUT THE AUTHOR
REBECCA DOBBINS

Rebecca (Becca) Dobbins holds a Master's in International Humanitarian Action and has a story that twists and turns through more than 92 countries, and wide-ranging occupational fields. After experimenting with event planning and ski instructing, she found passion and purpose working with the United Nations and other international organizations for over a decade, helping individuals affected by conflict and natural disasters.

More recently, she traded humanitarian work for a more direct people-centered approach, helping others transition and find their passion in life as a Certified Master Professional Coach. She believes each of these diverse experiences catapulted her to the next, each helping her to create her dream life. Today, Becca motivates and inspires others with her grit, and unwavering love of life, to seek out their dreams too.

She is a co-author of the Amazon bestselling book *You Matter: How women reclaiming their power are changing the world*. Her online coaching business is the winner of the 2021 "Best of Best" award in her hometown, and she serves clients all over the world.

You can connect with Becca at *www.sisuconceptcoaching.com* or via email *sisuconceptcoaching@gmail.com*.

Linkedin: *www.linkedin.com/in/rebecca-dobbins-1b5593a2*

SARA LIGHT

THE MAGIC OF CHAOS

There is magic everywhere, even in chaos.

I didn't always feel this way. For over a decade I'd felt that chaos had total control over my life.

In 2011 I was living in my home country of Spain, a beautiful sunny place that unfortunately had a culture and system I never resonated with. The city I was brought up in was a place where people would laugh at you when you had dreams, where making a living out of your passion seemed too good to be true, where your biggest goal was to get ANY job and keep it for as long as you could, even under precarious conditions, so that you could just about pay your bills. And that was it.

I recall spending my last year back home hiding in my room during the weekend, or behind my sunglasses and earphones when I had to leave the house. I was bored with explaining to enquiring strangers that my tattoos or piercings didn't mean I followed a questionable lifestyle or did drugs, that I was in fact the nerd from their kids' classrooms as I've always spent 99% of my spare time studying or watching documentaries ever since I was little.

Apparently, having tattoos made me look like some sort of criminal.

After handing in more CVs than I can even remember, I finally managed to find a job and work some shifts here and there at pubs and bars for under 4€ an hour. Everyone around me thought I was lucky to "at least have a job" and don't get me wrong, I was grateful for having a job too. But I didn't want to spend the rest of my life unceasingly chasing underpaying jobs until the age of 65, only to continue struggling with an unrealistic retirement plan whilst watching my body decay … honestly, no thanks.

That life lacked direction and purpose.

It was chaos.

Sweet & Salty Feelings

I always knew I wasn't made for that life. I knew there had to be more. And when I say more, I don't only mean more income, but more purpose, more recognition, more respect, more joy, more dreams, more LIFE. In 2011, after my first year at university studying English Translation & Interpreting, I managed to save 700€ from the bar jobs and, taking a leap of faith, I moved to London.

With that budget in one of the most expensive cities in the world, you can probably imagine that I only had one shot. I gave myself one month to find a job so that I could stay permanently in promising, buzzy London.

As I landed in the wet, foggy city, a heavy rain started to pour all over me. I remember crying my eyes out from pure joy, full of hope, as I felt my salty tears being washed away by the sweet raindrops of rainy London.

I made it.

I-bloody-made-it!

That was my first time in the UK. I was 21 and everything was completely new to me. I could barely speak English and I had no idea what a pound or a penny looked like. Also, despite studying English Translation & Interpreting at university for a year before I moved to the UK, it didn't take me long to notice that I couldn't understand the London accent!

Transitions

Completely ignoring the excitement of moving to a city that was 13 times larger in population than the one I came from, with all that entails, I left sightseeing for a later time. I focused on applying for all the jobs I could during my first two weeks in London. If I didn't apply for a couple of hundred jobs in under two weeks, I was very close to it.

How much fun!

What was fun was the non-stop calls and emails responding to my applications inviting me for interviews.

Back in my home country, speaking my mother tongue, I could wait for months and sometimes years (yes, years) before I received a reply to a job application. Now I was flooded with more interviews than I could fit in a month. I was blown away. This made me realise that there was so much to learn and this confirmed that there was more out there for me.

When I landed my first-ever job (another bar job ... but hey!) I was over the moon and almost hugged the manager and the owner as they gave me the news. Thankfully, I realised right in time that a hug wouldn't be socially acceptable! I don't think they'd ever seen anyone get so happy at being offered a £6/hour job. Apparently I did an amazing job during my interview and trial shift, although all I remember is responding 'yes' and nodding with a happy smile to everything I didn't understand, and I didn't understand A LOT of things.

Looking back, I must have looked like a complete nutcase.

As soon as I was offered the job, I called my best friend and guess what ... I burst out crying. Again. Remember my salty tears from when I landed? Well, they ran down my face very poetically once more, this time without rain. During those weeks I probably cried out of joy more than I've ever done in my whole life.

Fast forward a month, I was made an Assistant Manager at the bar.

A year later I was managing two branches and two teams of 20+ people. I was hiring, training people, helping with store openings, saving money and making friends. This was fun.

I was also working 15+ hours a day and sometimes didn't have a day off in two months. This wasn't fun. So I started planning my next chapter.

After more than two years managing teams, learning conflict resolution and employee relations, I grew a huge interest for Human Resources (HR), so this seemed like the natural next step in my career. Going from working at a bar to working in HR wasn't an easy journey and, despite getting some interviews, I was getting rejected from all of them. But I never gave up. It took me almost a year of constantly applying to every single HR vacancy I found and going to all the interviews only to get rejected: there was always someone with more experience than me, which wasn't difficult!

It was exhausting, I am not going to lie.

Until …

Fast forward one year. Whilst working at the bar I got a call.

I locked myself in the bathroom.

One of the largest (if not THE largest) architecture firms IN THE WORLD gave me my first HR job.

And let me tell you …

Life was fun again.

Cosmos Vs Chaos

I think at that stage I probably had bruises all over my arm from pinching myself so many times.

From struggling to get sporadic jobs under precarious conditions to working in London, in HR, in an office that shone more than Swarovski's storefront.

How did I make that happen?

I was so happy. Learned so much. Grew unimaginably. Got salary increases and bonuses every year. Got promoted. Kept learning …

I married the love of my life. Went on the longest honeymoon in Greece. Bought my first property with my wife … We were planning for a baby… we were so in love with each other. I had it all.

Or had I?

I got cheated on… (With a good friend of mine that happened to get married a month before.)

I got divorced …

I quit my job …

CHAOS

More Is Mess

It wasn't until I understood chaos and learned how to play with it that I started making REAL magic happen.

But it took me over a decade and a lot of pain to understand that chaos is a blessing. Chaos appears when you most need it, and sometimes that means when you feel you have it all. It appears not to destroy, but to rejuvenate the waters.

In astrology, water represents emotions. But the vessel (me) that held the water (my emotions) at some point started to look so sad that I stopped recognising myself in pictures. I disliked the way I looked in them so much that I refused to have any taken. My expression had started to shift a long time ago and I hadn't even noticed. After so many years fighting for a better life and transforming my journey inside out in such a short period of time, I didn't recognise myself.

Who was that?

And when did my eyebrows start to droop making me look like I was about to cry in every single picture?

I was shocked.

But then I realised that a long time ago I had entered a loop where all my days were just the repetition of the day before. I had so much stability, I had become so comfortable that I was holding the same water for many years. Now this water was getting murky. It actually started to smell so bad that in a matter of months after noticing, I just couldn't hold it anymore.

I started pouring the water out of the vessel. I started removing all the layers that were now stale and had hardened so much that I felt trapped in a dried-up case that didn't fit me anymore. It was keeping me tiny inside of it.

Becoming aware of this immediately activated a process that was too late for me to stop at that point. I would step onto the train to go to work and I would have a breakdown, crying my eyes out with so much anxiety. How was this possible? What was wrong with me? Come on, I was on my way to the same shiny office that one day changed my life, the one that believed in me and gave me a brand-new career in HR, allowing me to take a big leap.

Whilst they had given me my first HR role, I eventually felt like I was giving them more than I was receiving – I was giving them my precious time. I wasn't living. Leaving the house at 7am only to get back home knackered after 7pm was not living. Dragging Sundays, dreading Mondays, longing Fridays … was not living.

Once again, but for a very different reason, I asked myself: How did I make that happen?

I had been existing in that lifestyle for so long that all my senses were numb. I also didn't even notice all the physical illnesses I'd been suffering. The area under my eyes had darkened and were swollen, my facial expression had completely changed, I was constantly tired or ill which was rare for me ... And all of this was also reflected emotionally and intellectually. I was easily irritable and I used to forget so many things. I lacked focus.

The moment I realised how long I had ignored my situation; I had a huge awakening.

How long had I been numb?

Going to work was a mission. Getting out of bed and showering or cooking also became a mission and I had lost track of the time I'd been feeling like that. I just knew I needed to do something about it. I didn't blame anyone or anything. I have always been aware that I'd chosen the life I wanted to live, I always did. The same way I chose my partner, my jobs, the countries I lived in, the friends I made ... and whilst I was forever grateful for all the choices I'd made and all the people I'd met during my journey, I understood that perhaps I needed to reassess my life.

I needed to heal.

The Awakening

My marriage wasn't going very well either. After I found out about the cheating and my marriage was broken, I felt so lost. Without any sense of direction, I felt like I had no control over my life. It took this situation to make me realise that I had been in a toxic, co-dependent relationship that was making us both extremely unhappy.

Little did I know that this divorce would be the biggest blessing I've ever experienced, along with quitting my job due to the extreme burnout.

Once I quit my last corporate job, I wasn't physically capable to work a 9 to 5 again. A massive healing period was due and I was determined to get better.

I'd been numb for so many years, then went through a divorce and quit my job without a plan B. This all made me feel like I was nowhere near healing and, even worse, I had no clue where to start.

One thing I knew for sure. After removing so many layers and leaving so many aspects of my life behind, I was becoming a blank canvas and now I had to repaint my whole life, redesigning my whole being again. I simply couldn't be the one I was before. Even if I could, I didn't want to.

Removing what didn't serve me was a relief. But what was I supposed to do with the blank canvas that remained?

Where should I get the paint from?

What colours did I want to paint with?

Which shapes did I like?

I had no idea.

A couple of years before my marriage went down the drain, I was visiting my sister-in-law, and whilst having a drink in her garden, she started talking about crystals. She told me about how they have their own vibration, like all rocks do – even wood, plants and everything on this Earth. I remember feeling something moving inside me, a feeling of goosebumps.

As a kid, I used to keep little stones and sticks as amulets and carry them around to give me luck and protection. I believed in magic and I understood the power of chaos.

That memory sparked so much in the coming months and years. As an adult I had simply stopped practising my rituals. I had forgotten that magic exists and the weight of the layers I started wearing eventually made me drag my feet around.

I realised that whilst I couldn't and didn't want to go back to being "the old Sara", I did have to go back to basics and remember my essence. Bringing back memories of my childhood helped in this process and so I started playing.

I played with life and explored all the things that felt right:

- I needed to generate income but couldn't go to a physical office anymore, so I registered as self-employed and started working remotely on Graphic Design and HR projects for clients. Being able to work my own hours and to choose who to work with gave me the freedom and space I was craving. I found a way to sustain myself financially whilst I figured life out.

- Practising Yoga gave a structure to my day and my mind, so I went on to study my 200-hour Yoga Teacher Training. I completed it and continued with my 500-hour. Studying the Philosophy of Yoga and exploring Yoga as a different career option widened my horizons in a way that nothing else had before.

- My mind was constantly overthinking, and I had heard of that thing called meditation, so I gave it a go. It worked. It worked so well that I stuck to it. I still practise it today and I never miss a practice like I never miss brushing my teeth. Keeping your mental hygiene is as important as keeping your personal hygiene. Would you go about your day with poor hygiene? Same goes for your mind.

- After all that drama I realised I had eaten my body weight in all the food I could find and ended up 15 kg heavier. Those 15 extra kg that I was carrying around, feeling heavy and lazy, were gone after a few months of workouts and healthy diet. But more importantly, I make sure they don't return by keeping a good daily mental hygiene.

- I started my own coaching business as a Spiritual Life Facilitator and I now guide Seekers in the transition from trading their time for money to awakening and discovering their Higher Purpose. To create their own Business, Freedom & Wealth and live a life based on their terms.

The Higher Purpose Collective

I have learned (and continue learning) how to play with chaos.
But you can only afford to play with chaos when you know what cosmos feels like.

Did you know that the opposite of chaos is cosmos?

Cosmos is a Greek word for the order of the Universe. It defines a very complex but well-ordered system, like the Universe. Or like our minds when we make sure we've done our daily hygiene.

We live in a constant switch between both, and none is better than the other:

- Living in cosmos is necessary when there is way too much going on in your life
- Switching to chaos is necessary when you feel stagnant and need to make progress

Get too comfortable, and you will cultivate murky waters.

Get too messy and you will have no water to cultivate.

Chaos once took over my life, simply because I got distracted and forgot to bring back a little bit of cosmos.

This is a reminder that you've been born in this exact lifetime with the mission to accomplish something BIG. Take this as a sign to start exploring your Higher Purpose, because nobody has been put on this Earth to pay bills whilst getting depleted in the process.

The great news is that what you're here to accomplish isn't "just" being able to pay for a ridiculously high rent whilst saving, meditating, drinking your water, doing your daily workout and what-not. As energy beings, we have a Higher Purpose to fulfil.

When you get lost, start playing. There is nothing wrong in exploring all the things you are curious about to bring the spark back into your life. Get comfortable with being uncomfortable and welcome the chaos into your life because you only ever attract what you are truly ready for.

ABOUT THE AUTHOR
SARA LIGHT

Sara Light is a Life Purpose Facilitator, Yoga Teacher and Astrologer.

She helps Seekers transition from trading time for money to creating their own, Freedom & Wealth by fulfilling their Higher Purpose. She uses ancient practices like Yoga & Pranayama as well as NLP techniques to re-programme the collective's minds into their most authentic estate.

After 11+ years in the corporate world, Sara experienced a powerful awakening in 2017 which led her to quit her job. Having suffered from severe burnout and anxiety as a consequence of living a life that wasn't for her, she now guides others to remember their Higher Purpose, using the power of Rituals & Tribe.

Sara also lives her purpose through painting, sculpting, reading Tarot, dancing and studying Astrology.

Website: *www.iamsaralight.com/defaultsite*
Facebook: *www.facebook.com/groups/iamsaralight*
Instagram: *www.instagram.com/iamsaralight*
Email: *hello@iamsaralight.com*

SARAH B. BLAKE

BURNING THE BOXES

It's not stress:

Ten days after my 40th birthday, I was in a cylindrical box getting my brain scanned.

As they strapped me in, giving me directions that I needed to stay perfectly still for the scans to work, all I could think was, *My ADD brain is going to have fun with this.*

As the whirl of the machine started, I could hear my rapid heartbeat in my ears.

In between wandering thoughts of the list of things I needed to get done, the disastrous stories I was telling myself about what this was, I tried to calm myself down and thought, *Well, at least you'll have some answers after this.*

I heard them say, "Ok, we're going to start the eight-minute scan now."

Crap, I thought the last one was the long one, and the machine whirled to life once again.

Deep. Slow. Calming. Breaths. Nope. That's not working. How much time is left?

And then three words came to me: *Gratitude. Present. Create. States of being to live my life. Be in a state of gratitude. Be present. Create the life I want. Gratitude. Present. Create.*

Those three words kept me as calm as possible inside that cylindrical box.

I thought I had Multiple Sclerosis (MS) or a brain tumor. I had all sorts of symptoms: tingly hands, vertigo, dizziness, crazy sensitivity to what I can only describe as offending odors, pressure on the back left side of my head that I swore housed a hard mass that the right side didn't have, and the cognitive recall issues. That's one that really started to scare me, not the twitching of the eye, or increased soreness in the jaw from uncontrollable clenching, especially in my sleep.

It was the cognitive issues that had me scared. For example, I knew the word I wanted to use, and it started with the letter "J", and the word "June" would come out when I really meant to say "January". That was happening more and more frequently, and it was scary as hell.

After about six months of paying a little more attention to all of the symptoms it was time for me to find a primary care doctor who would be my central hub for figuring out what was going on. After 45 minutes of asking me questions regarding my symptoms, lifestyle, and work, the doctor thought it could be one of three things: thyroid, MS or stress. I laughed and quickly dismissed stressed. I had been in the same job for a while; I was used to the culture I was working in. Granted we had a big new event happening. I was leading the project – we would have a booth and announce a new product line. But no, it could not be stress. I told the doctor I was getting my brain scanned, and I was only at his office so one place could hold all of my medical records as I was going to figure this out. This was something medical. Not stress.

And so my medical journey began. It started with initial bloodwork and the brain scan. I met with several neurologists, a rheumatologist, neck and spine doctors, dermatologists, a hematologist, and other specialists. I had more blood work done. My immune system seemed to be crashing. My doctor asked me once again about my life in general and work. Again, I insisted this couldn't be stress.

Around this same time at work, I finally decided to speak up and advocate for myself. I had been in the same job title and pay range for over three years, and had taken on not only an increasing workload, but work that had decision-making authority that impacted the profit-and-loss centers of the organization. During that review cycle I had not received the promotion I knew I had earned so, in true character, I investigated and didn't relent. What I found out was shocking. I compared my current position in the organization to the work I had been doing for well over two years. I was three grades below where I should be.

With my heart racing, anxious to speak up for myself and coming up against the conditioning of what we are told not to do – Don't brag; Don't rock the boat; Don't talk about yourself – I presented the case for why I had earned a promotion. I asked my manager, if he didn't agree with me, what I needed to do to make it happen. I could feel my chest tightening, heart beating even faster, as I waited for his response to my well thought out justification, with visual aids, to justify the reason for my request. I even used language he could understand – military language, as he was a retired aviator. Summary: I was doing the work of an officer, but I was being compensated as enlisted personnel.

Instead of being met with an appreciation for an employee advocating for themselves, wanting to "climb the corporate ladder", taking ownership (you know, all of things that are written by the human resources department outlining how employees are "supposed to act") I was met with resistance and annoyance. Management seemed surprised, which was odd considering I would have "Jill of All Trades" or "Bulldog – won't let go and gets the hard work done" on my reviews.

I was asked why I wanted the promotion as I would never be the director of the group I was in. Wow, I'm not sure what I was expecting, but it wasn't this.

"Um, because I am doing the work at this level, have been doing the work at that level, and would like to be compensated accordingly. Can we talk about my career growth plan once this is resolved?"

That was not the response he was looking for. In speaking up for myself I was shining an unwelcome spotlight on him. A spotlight that confirmed he was not a good manager or leader of people. He had not been doing his job: THREE paygrades, and years of this going unnoticed by him. There was such a large disparity that the Vice President of the organization and the Vice President of Human Resources got involved.

I had a great track record.

I had consistently earned above average reviews.

I had been handpicked to work on a program with complicated customers, multiple funding sources and a hardware demonstration at a military base, in a restricted area.

I had been quickly singled out as an "emerging leader" within my division, and the company.

I got my Master of Science in Organizational Leadership & Development.

I was learning to be more politically savvy in an office environment, or so I thought.

I was stepping out from under people who claimed to be my mentors, as I was carving out my own career path.

It took months for the promotion to be approved. But the damage had been done. I was not viewed in good light for having stood up for myself and my manager placed me in the "she's money hungry" box to anyone that would listen.

I had rocked the boat.

The older, apparently wiser, male leaders viewed me as "junior support" and that was where they wanted me to stay.

Seven months later, for the first time, I had a "mid-year" review two months before regular reviews. Although he tried to hide it, there was glee on my manager's face as he told me all the things I was doing wrong. He was so sure this would crush me. It wasn't a secret that I thrived on one-on-one positive feedback. Now he was using my own words against me, words that I had used to describe the poor behaviors of others. I was "condescending. Not a team player. Not collaborative." Seven months earlier my review was quite the opposite.

Was this really happening? He knew I was single, with a mortgage, with no second income or person to fall back on. He was going to control me into submission with the job, my paycheck, my livelihood as his leverage to stop me from speaking up against the condescending and sexist behaviors of my counterparts, and of his.

I was shocked that he thought he could get away with this … but he knew he could. And he did.

As the "dressing down" (in military terms) continued, he concluded with, "Not a lot of positive. Surprising, isn't it?" When I looked up from my notes, I could see him holding back a smile. He was so proud of himself for ripping me apart. Although I knew what he was saying wasn't true, it still hurt. I knew my behaviors didn't align with what he was saying. I also knew that they didn't reflect any of the written feedback he had received. I was panicking inside. My heart raced, the lump swelled in my throat as I tried to answer his question, which was really a statement.

"Yes, it is surprising. Can I see this feedback?"

"No."

"Did any women give feedback?"

Wow. He did not like that question. I was supposed to be cowering in the corner after that dressing down, instead I had the audacity to ask that question.

191

In a defensive tone he responded, "Would that make a difference?"

"I don't know. Just curious."

It was a valid question. My colleagues were mainly men. I was typically the only female in most meetings. Usually, the youngest looking.

"You have a lot to think about, don't you? And how you're going to act differently?"

Looking over my notes, as he didn't give me a copy of anything, I could only respond with, "Yes, there is a lot here."

I could feel the tears coming to the surface. The knot in my throat grew, and a new one formed in my stomach. I quickly walked the short distance from his office to mine and closed the door. I was shaking as I was trying to gather my things so I could get out of there as quickly as I could.

I had to escape from this madness.

I had to get away.

I had to move quicker.

Don't cry. Don't cry. Not yet. You can cry on the way home.

These were not tears of sadness. These were tears of anger, of rage. Tears of generations of women having to put up with this manipulating bullshit, the inexcusable behavior of men that think that they are entitled to control, shame, and weaken any women who is perceived as going against them.

I clenched my jaw and fought the urge to run.

Pack your stuff up. Deep breath. Stay calm. Cry later. Don't ...

There was a loud knock, knock on my door.

Deep breath. Please don't have a shaky, weak voice.

"Yes".

My manager popped his head in with a little grin, "Yes, 'Jane' gave feedback."

He closed the door.

'Jane' was a former military pilot in a leadership position at the same level as my manager.

Her office was on the way to mine.

He was covering his ass.

He was closing ranks.

I didn't fully realize it at the time, but that's when the group retaliation and gaslighting had officially begun. He was not shy and didn't try to hide what he was doing. He didn't need to. The company culture had allowed this behavior from others before, they will allow it again.

I got out of there as quickly as I could, fighting the urge to cry, to scream or to throw up. As I started my car, the tears came rushing down. I couldn't breathe. I thought I was going to start hyperventilating. My stomach was joining the churn of emotions. The lump in my throat couldn't decide whether it wanted to be swallowed or to be ejected out.

By this point I had come close to realizing I was fucked.

This is when I began not wearing eye makeup when I knew I had to have a one-on-one meeting with my manager. I made sure they were scheduled in the afternoons, so I could head home immediately after the meeting. He was manipulating and twisting everything around to make it suit his narrative – I was a 'problem employee'. And there was nothing I could do about it. He had made sure to close ranks around him; made sure their narratives would come close to matching his narrative.

I was officially in the box of "problem employee that won't be controlled".

A different manager tried to be helpful and asked me why I couldn't just keep my head down. "If you need to take a demotion, just do it. At least you'd still have a job."

My only response was, "Because it's wrong. It's not ok."

At the time, I didn't see this as an option. I needed to stand up for myself and for any of the other people who felt like their circumstances wouldn't allow them to speak up. Taking a demotion, keeping my mouth shut, just finding another job elsewhere – these were not options. I was doing everything right. I was not the problem; they were.

Not only were things changing for me at work but my health was becoming a big concern. We weren't any closer to finding out what was going on with me medically. About a month later my doctor thought it would be good to take some time away and try to get my immune system back in order. And maybe I should start seeing a psychotherapist, you know, just in case it is stress.

In retrospect:

I was consistently put in other people's boxes.

From a young age I was put in the boxes of:

Don't talk so much.
Don't be such a screw up.
Don't embarrass me.
Don't be so weird.
Don't be such a tomboy.

And as I hit my high-school and college age, the boxes grew to include:

Don't be such a leader.
Don't be so friendly.
Don't talk so much. (Got that one a lot.)
Don't try so hard.
Don't be so curious.

Although I didn't like it, I wanted to fit in. So I kept trying to be smaller, trying to fit myself into the boxes others had made for me.

Professionally it became the boxes of contradictions:
Don't be so nice. (You won't be a good manager.)
Don't be so serious, it's just a job.
Don't smile too much. (The men will think you're flirting with them.)
Don't ask so many questions. Don't assume you know the answers.
Don't be so stand-offish. It's ok for male counterparts to push back on support functions, but not you as you won't be viewed as a team player.
Don't sit quietly in meetings but don't speak up or it will look like you're trying to take over.

… it just doesn't stop! Although it's a system, a game if you will, that women are not set up to win, I kept trying. I really tried.

In the spirit of trying, I decided I just needed to get more education to prove I knew what I was talking about professionally. I got a second Master's less than three years after finishing my first. Upon asking my manager which program he would recommend (as he would need to sign off on tuition reimbursement), I received a note on one of the program information sheets – "I think this program is more relevant to the working girl, 2nd less credits to complete."

Um, what? Working girl? Is this really how little he thinks of me? Of women in general? It's one thing to think it. It's something else to not try to hide it, but to write it out as well.

This brings us back to when I realized I couldn't ignore my health issues and I had to get my brain scanned.

I decided I would need to postpone the second Master's and concentrate on my health. When my doctor recommended I take time off, I sent an email to my manager telling him that I would be taking FMLA (Family Medical Leave Act) to work on my health. He was out of town on a work trip when he received it. He didn't realize I was friends with one of the people that were with him. He had no qualms about hiding his thoughts and said out loud to the people around him, "Oh look, Sarah is taking time off to go get her head fixed." When I heard this was how my manager reacted, my heart started racing again. The tears of anger started to rise up. So much anxiety.

How could I be the problem with this sort of behavior around me? They were.

Turns out, I was the problem. Why? Because I spoke up. I stood up for myself. I called out the behaviors the company said they don't tolerate. I had unintentionally pointed out the issues that women face every day within organizations like this. You see, if they agreed that my manager was a problem, then they would have to look at the other people around him who exhibited the same behaviors. And then they would have to look at the entire organization. And then the entire company.

So yes, I was the problem. A problem for them that was easily solved. A problem for me that was damaging on so many levels.

Many people would say I had/have anger, so much anger about what happened to me. Maybe it was to begin with, but within six months it wasn't anger. I had seen a psychotherapist (doctor's orders) during the last eight months at that company. I was frustrated that everyone kept telling me I was angry when I wasn't. I was passionate to make sure that what was happening to women 40 years ago and was happening to me now should be stopped and wouldn't continue in the future.

196

About a year and a half after I left the corporate life and had just been laid off from a two-person training and development company, I was finally looking to my network for the next step for me career wise. I had avoided networking for so long. For the last two years at the company, I was in denial. Denial that I was in fight or flight. Denial around how long things had been off. Denial that the only solution for the company was for me to be gone: gone from my department; gone from the organization; gone from the company. It didn't matter to them, as long as I was gone.

It wasn't until someone, who I didn't know very well at the time, made a statement. She didn't tell me I was angry or that I needed therapy. She calmly reflected, "Sarah, you have the language of someone who has experienced a lot of trauma. A lot of unresolved trauma."

Wow. That hit.

That hit home.

And hard.

Being seen.

Being heard.

It was no surprise to me that this woman had worked in the technology field and didn't need to know any details to know there was trauma that I hadn't even acknowledged. I spent the next nine months "detoxing". Detoxing from the lies; from the isolation; that they were able to get away with what they did; from the consistent reminder I was "lucky to be doing the work I was, as it wasn't a real job anyway"; from the company culture of rewarding poor behavior.

Coming to this realization was hard. It meant that I had spent the last five years at a job that I thought I loved, a job that I allowed to define me as a person, define my success, define my worth, in fight or flight mode. I was living in stress so much every day I couldn't see it.

My Success Box:

I left my corporate life, not as a Corporate Dropout turned aspirational entrepreneur, living my life's purpose.

No, I consider myself a Corporate Refugee.

I fought to stay.

I fought for what I thought was right.

I eventually left the job with the help of lawyers.

Ultimately my body knew better than my mind. My body knew I would not survive, much less thrive, in that culture. It took my body shutting down for me to take a step back, to pause and reflect on my situation. If this had not happened, I would have kept making excuses and "powering through it". If not at that particular organization/company, I would have repeated the cycle at another corporate job.

Being a Corporate Refugee has had its struggles. Financially I'm not where I would like to be. Not even close. It's taken a couple of years to figure out what I want my business to be and how to talk about it. I'm still shifting as I learn new concepts that I think would help my clients.

A single income with a mortgage can make career choices even more stressful. But I can honestly say that despite the uncertainty of financial situations, I have not once felt the stress, anxiety, panic, shame, incompetence, as I did when I was at my corporate job, much less the consistency of that stress. I'm told I look different, more confident, happier, healthier than before. I even had a former colleague say she didn't recognize me in a picture I had on social media.

It's because I wasn't allowed to shine at that job.

My definition of success has shifted since leaving corporate; it took years to detox from the lies of corporate environment's version of what success should be.

For me, success isn't about the job title, making six figures, the next promotion.

Success is finding alignment. Alignment of my values, my stories (not the stories of the 'shoulds' from someone else) and my surroundings.

Success is coaching others to find their alignment and watching them flourish on their terms.

Success is not living in anyone else's boxes.

Success is living in the expansive "boxes" of self-care, self-advocacy, self-love and boundaries.

ABOUT THE AUTHOR
SARAH B. BLAKE

Sarah Blake is CEO and founder of Sarah Blake Consulting focusing on Emotional Intelligence & Leadership coaching. She works with individuals and companies utilizing coaching, trainings/facilitation, and consulting strategies to reinforce growth.

Core to her personal and professional life, is the belief that when there is alignment with our stories, values and surroundings, there is alignment within.

Co-creating possibilities with her clients is what drives her.

For over 20 years, she held many different titles in the corporate world: business development, strategic marketing, and human resources, to name a few.

She has an M.S. in Organizational Leadership & Development, has professional certificates across many disciplines, as well as being a founding member of The Global Institute for Thought Leadership.

She is an ICF ACC coach affiliated with the ACC as an Emotional Intelligence and Leadership coach.

She resides in Colorado, with her dog(s) – depending on if there are foster dogs in the house or not.

You can connect with Sarah at *www.sarahblakeconsulting.com*

Linkedin: *www.linkedin.com/in/sarahblake*
Facebook: *www.facebook.com/sarahblakeconsulting*

TARRYN REEVES

THE DECISION TO CHOOSE JOY

When I was growing up I was always told by those around me what an 'acceptable' job was. If I wasn't being told outright, it was obvious from the way those with 'less acceptable' jobs were treated, spoken about and paid. Like a potter with expert hands subtly but firmly pushing us into a form deemed beautiful and worthy of being, society moulds us from the moment we are born. And so we continually strive to become that which we are told is worthy of us.

We may think that we have evolved far beyond our caveman and cavewoman ways. To some extent we have but our basic biology and internal wiring remains much the same. The need to fit in and be accepted by the 'tribe' is hardwired into our brains. Being banished from our tribe could quite literally mean death for us. It was hard, almost impossible, to survive on your own in that early environment and part of the survival instinct is to stay in harmony with the tribe.

It takes courage to stand on your own and go against the flow. It takes resilience to keep getting up when circumstances knock you down. It takes grit to stay true to your chosen path. It takes determination to do what you know can be done when those around you are telling you it can't.

This is the story of my journey from innocent child to society's puppet, becoming a Corporate Dropout and making the decision to choose joy and create a life on my own terms. Join me as I reflect on the common path that so many of us take when trying to find our place in the world. Who knows, this may be the very thing that finally gives you the courage to take the leap and soar to new heights.

Childhood

I was born in Zimbabwe, Africa, in 1987. My life was full of amazing adventures most kids only see in the movies. Camping under a sky full of the brightest stars every other weekend. Running barefoot through the land that ran for miles in every direction. Climbing trees and rocks to build forts and bring to life imaginary castles. Seeing zebra, kudu, impala and warthog was an everyday occurrence. My childhood was magical.

I was also surrounded by extreme differences in class. The majority of wealthy people owned farms, ran businesses, worked in big corporations or for the government and some didn't need to work at all. At the other end of the spectrum there were gardeners, maids, cleaners, cooks and those who worked on the farms. This is not a story about race – not today. I simply want to highlight the vast range of people I knew.

When asked what I wanted to be when I grew up, I always replied that I wanted to be a game ranger or a vet. While the vet was the more 'acceptable' choice as a game ranger was more middle class, in my heart the game ranger was my deepest desire. I couldn't bear to have to put animals to sleep as a vet – I would most likely be more upset than the pet owner!

Alas my journey was not to continue on this path, and I was forced to make a rather dramatic turn when political violence tore my home apart and we were forced to flee. At the age of 15 I moved to Australia in January 2003 with my family.

Adolescence

Making the move to Australia at such a critical time of growth in my life was unsettling to say the least. I had been bullied at school and had grown to be the weird one among my peers. Weird because I did things my way and wasn't concerned with what was trending and what wasn't. I just did me and peer pressure was like water off a duck's back when it came to my decision-making.

There was, however, a part deep inside of me that was yearning to be liked and accepted. I was tired of the constant bullying and behind-the-back comments about how different I was. When my parents told me we were moving I wrote in my diary: 'When I move to Australia, I am going to become someone that everyone likes.' And I did.

I was liked by my peers. Drank too much. I slipped into the different roles like an award-winning actress with every new boyfriend that came along. I did this crazy chameleon shape-shifting dance so many times that eventually I fooled my brain into believing that it was the real deal. I completely forgot who I truly was, what I stood for, what I wanted and enslaved myself to the societal dance of acceptability. I was palatable to society and that was safe and comfortable.

This is a dangerous game to play as many never make it back out. The ancient wisdom of the body and soul know better and will bring you crashing back to reality if you don't come back willingly. And so it was with me.

Young Adulthood

Going to university was something that was never a question in my family. From the moment I was born it was expected that I would work hard to achieve great things in my life and it was assumed that I couldn't possibly do any of that unless I went to university and got a degree in an 'approved' field.

Again, I toyed with the idea of becoming a vet but the stark truth that I would never be able to willingly kill an animal (and why I am now a vegetarian) made me choose a different path. I considered so many options, including creative ones, which were promptly put on the 'blacklist' by my parents who only wanted the best for me. Eventually I settled on studying Radiation Therapy (the practice of using radiation to kill and shrink cancer cells) as it would allow me to help people, earn a great income and 'step up' in the world. I loved the study but when it came to practical placement in a real hospital, I realised that this was definitely not something I could do long term. While at the Prince of

Wales Hospital in Sydney, we treated many children with cancer from the neighbouring children's hospital. Radiation therapy treatment involves many repeat sessions and so I got to know my patients well during our time together. Seeing children, many of whom were dying, come in day after day for a treatment that made them feel so sick was soul destroying. We would often get appointments cancelled as a child had passed away during the night. I just couldn't do it. My heart was hurting. So six months before graduating I decided to make a change and began looking at other options.

I decided on studying for a Bachelor of Criminology via distance education so that I could get a full-time job and earn money to buy my own house while also earning my degree. I loved being able to study online as it meant I could utilise my time more efficiently and get on the road to success faster. Do more. Achieve more. Work harder. Success at any cost. These were the subconscious messages that played on a constant reel inside me.

I applied for a job as a Crewing Support Officer in the railway. I didn't have half of the skills they were asking for but the salary was very attractive and I knew that I could learn anything I put my mind to and so I applied. I got the job.

I loved the fast-paced environment of the Live Run room. No two days (or nights) were the same and there was always a problem to solve. The delicate balance of crewing the trains was a giant puzzle that was constantly moving and morphing. I was good at it.

I never planned to stay in the railway but to save up as much money as possible from my lucrative new job, finish my Criminology degree and become a forensic detective. The Universe had other plans. One day my future husband limped into the office on crutches after a weekend motorbike accident. I looked up from my desk and thought to myself, 'That guy has a cute butt!' Recovering from a recent breakup from my long-term boyfriend I was looking to alleviate my pain by having my first-ever one-night stand. I felt like I was being too structured, too 'nice girl', so that was my foolish remedy for my perceived flaws. Turns out I really suck at the whole one-night stand thing as that guy never left! 11 years later we are happily married with a beautiful daughter.

My husband was a train driver and also earned good money. That was great but it also meant we couldn't just pack up and move to a city where Criminology was actually considered a job – there are no Criminology jobs in Newcastle. I made the decision to choose love and so stayed working in the railway. This was my first real decision to start climbing the corporate ladder.

Although I loved the job, the toxic environment of the office soon began to eat away at my big heart. There were two older women who just seemed incapable of being nice. No matter what I did I felt like they couldn't stand me. For a people pleaser like me, that really hurt. They would bring in biscuits and offer them around the three-person office and exclude me. They would say nasty things and never had anything but criticism of my work. My boss was aware of the problem but unfortunately did not have the courage needed to lead people effectively. Perhaps I was just being too sensitive? I became more and more unhappy and had no idea what to do about it. The money was too good to leave behind.

One lunchtime as I was licking my wounds after another round with one of the office staff, I got a call from a train driver who used to work with the company. He had left to join a competitive rail provider and told me that he had spoken to the owners of this relatively new company about my skills. They wanted to know if I would be interested in coming in for an interview. My heart soared! YES! This was my way out! Surely the grass is greener on the other side.

I landed a job with that company and they really seemed to value me and my skillset. I was given the position of Crewing Support Officer again. As they were just starting out, they didn't have any procedures or real systems to follow so my job was to create and document them. I loved my colleagues and thrived in my new role. My ability to take up a position with nothing and create amazing procedures and foundations meant that I was soon promoted into other roles to do the same thing and finally ended up in the role of Rostering Officer. I had my own office in a fancy new building that overlooked Newcastle Harbour. I drove a new car. Went on overseas holidays every year. Travelled for work. Bought a house. Got the train to work every day, walked along the city street in my fancy business outfit, wheeling my business bag and stopping in at my favourite café to grab a coffee on the way to my successful corporate job. Yup, I had it made. At the age of 26 I was living the dream, baby! Or was I?

From all appearances, I had it all but as so often happens, we never know what goes on behind closed doors. The constant pressure and growing toxicity of my work environment was starting to wear me down. Part of my job involved approving or denying leave applications. This was done according to a very strict system with little room to move as we could not jeopardise the crewing plan for running our fleet. I would get daily phone calls from train crew members abusing me for denying their leave. They would hurl obscenities down the phone calling me all sorts of names, including 'cunt'. It got to the point that every time my phone rang, my heart would accelerate with anxiety. When I reported this to HR, I was told by the female department head, who was also co-owner of the company, that the abuse was likely due to the fact that I was a young girl with a foreign accent in a management position in a male-dominated industry and to more or less get over it. 'Perhaps you should try to speak more Australian,' she said.

Despite this, I loved working with my boss. I thought he was a great leader and looked up to him. We worked closely together and had a good working relationship. He worked from home some days and invited me to do the same so I started working from home once a week. I loved working from home as it gave me a break from the stale air conditioning, the blinding fluorescent lights and the constant chaos of the Live Run room. I grew more and more stressed and dreaded going to the office so I started working from home more. I never assumed that this arrangement had a caveat as it was never expressed. One day when I called my boss to advise him that I would be working from home that day, he started to yell at me. He was shouting at the top of his lungs, which was scary as hell. He said I was working from home too much and that I better get my arse into the office. From then on I was too scared to work from home.

As I was one of the very few women in the company working so closely with men all day, many of them seemed to think it was okay to make inappropriate sexual comments or flirt with me. If I showed any reaction, I was a 'bitch', but if I responded I was a 'whore'. The easiest thing to do was let it slide, which I did. I became so numb to this behaviour that it was only many years later that I realised just how horrible it is. One day when my boss told me that he didn't like the pants I was wearing to work, I asked him why. He replied, 'Because I liked your arse better in the skirt you were wearing yesterday.' I laughed and walked off, not thinking anything of it. Just another day in paradise.

The Descent into Darkness

I told myself that I had it made! I was successful. I had the house, the car, the boyfriend, the office, the salary … I had myself so convinced that I was doing life right that nobody knew that I was suffering, least of all me.

My face broke out in an unexplainable red rash that lasted for over a year. It was painful and embarrassing. My wedding was coming up and I was doing everything I could to get rid of this unsightly issue. I consulted doctors, skin specialists and naturopaths and even went on acne medication. Nothing worked. My boss had the audacity to suggest that it was stress. I laughed in his face. Me, stressed? Please! I wasn't weak and nothing could bring me down.

I woke every morning with an absolute feeling of dread coursing throughout my entire body and forced myself out of bed to get ready for work. I would give myself pep talks in the mirror about how fierce and strong I was. I'd apply my make-up telling myself it was war paint and that my clothes were armour as I prepared to fight the battle of my day ahead. I literally felt like I was a warrior going to war. Ready to fight at any cost.

I wasn't sleeping well, had no appetite and was losing weight (I am already tiny and cannot afford to lose any weight!). I was really losing my mind but I still had no idea.

My work phone would ring and my heart would accelerate, my breathing would seize and my palms would sweat.

I developed a constant shaking in my hands to the point where I was convinced I had some sort of Parkinson's disease.

My workplace offered free counselling sessions so I booked in. The counsellor told me that I had PTSD, chronic depression and major anxiety. He also told me that what I was experiencing at work was sexual harassment and that I should report it. I never went back to see him again.

I would wake several times a night convinced that I could see physical beings in my room. Nobody else could see them, which made them (and me) think that I was going crazy. It became a struggle to get out of bed in the morning and I was using alcohol to numb the pain. Still, I soldiered on.

I went to see several doctors about my increasing levels of fatigue, convinced that there was something wrong with me. How was it possible to be this fatigued and still able to function? There had to be an explanation. They checked my thyroid, my iron levels and everything else they could think of. Eventually my regular doctor (a South African lady, familiar with what I had experienced in Africa) sat me down and told me that I had breathing issues, chronic depression and major anxiety. She told me that she would like me to see a breathing specialist and go on medication to help me with the depression and anxiety.

My internal response:
What the hell is she on about?
I can breathe just fine thank you very much.
If I didn't know how to breathe then I would clearly be dead. Duh!
Who the fuck doesn't know how to breathe?!
There is no such thing as depression or anxiety. That is a made-up thing for people who can't get their shit together and handle life.

I stared at her and told her, 'I'm not going on medication and I certainly don't have depression or anxiety. I'm just tired is all. And of course I know how to breathe!'

She patiently explained the situation to me while I hysterically sobbed and argued with her that this couldn't possibly be true. I wasn't weak! I could do anything! She finally explained it to me in a way that I understood, convincing me to go on the medication, just to 'try it out'.

She told me that my mental health was like a mud hole and that I was a truck stuck in that mud, doing my best to get out but not able to on my own. She told me that the medication was like a tow truck that would hitch up to me and slowly pull me out of the hole. It would keep on towing me up the hill until I got to the top and then we could discuss coming off it. She said that if I quit the medication before reaching the top that I would continue to fall back down the hill and into the mud.

I agreed to go on the medication and decided to try yoga and meditation to see if that would help my breathing. I slowly began to feel better. I understood that I needed time to heal and so I quit my high-flying corporate job without a plan B.

I started doing casual work for various companies through an employment agency. When I was working as a Roster Clerk in a not-for-profit, they offered me a permanent position, which I happily accepted. Two weeks later there was a large internal restructure and I was told that my position was now redundant and that there would be no payout for me as I hadn't been there long enough. A week later I flew to the UK for a five week holiday that had been booked months previously. I figured I would look for another job when I got home.

A Reason to Change

On our road trip through the UK I took frequent naps in the car, which was unusual for me. When we reached the Lakes District I was bed bound in our B & B by what we thought was severe food poisoning. By the time we arrived in the Cotswolds I had missed my period so I headed down to the local pharmacy to get a pregnancy test. Lo and behold – I was pregnant.

In that moment, sitting in the bathroom of the fancy hotel looking at the positive result, everything else fell away and I had such clarity. I had to take control of my life and create something wonderful for my unborn child. I had to show him or her what was possible for them and model the change I wished to see in the world. I didn't want to play the victim anymore. I wanted to be the heroine for my baby. A fierce lioness energy settled deep within my bones.

I called my doctor in Australia and informed her that I had read about the side effects of the medication I was on and that I wasn't willing to take them for fear of harming my baby and that I would be quitting them immediately. She warned me profusely against quitting cold turkey as the consequences could be severe, but I was having none of it. The pills were flushed down the toilet that day.

On my return to Australia I tried to get another job but nobody would hire me because I was pregnant. I decided to stop looking and to take the time to heal and prepare for the arrival of my baby. I would look for a job after that.

Six weeks after my daughter, Autumn, was born, I came across a post on Facebook asking if anyone would be interested in doing some admin work for an essential oils business from home. I thought, *I can do that!*, and applied. I got the job and enjoyed using my intellect again. I did such a good job that referrals began to pour in. It suddenly hit me – why the hell should I go back and work for someone else? I can work for myself!

Life in This Moment

I guess you could call me an 'accidental entrepreneur' but I know I was always made to be one. Five years later and I am the proud leader of my three brands. Four Eagles Publishing is the publishing house for visionaries, disruptors and leaders. We are passionate about bringing to life books without altering or censoring the author's truth. Zimpasha is the creative marketing and virtual assistance agency supporting high-level entrepreneurs to get visible and scale their business to new heights. Tarryn Reeves is my personal brand under which I speak, write and teach about life, business, spirituality and everything in between. I built these businesses from scratch and designed my life according to how I wanted it to be.

It may look like life is easy and I have my shit together. Truth be told, I don't think anyone truly does! Life is a journey with ups, downs and sideways skids but oh what a joy to live and learn each and every day. Some days are easy. Some days are hard. Some days you get sucker punched in the gut so hard it brings you to your knees. The key is to find the courage to keep getting up and keep going no matter what is thrown your way. Enjoy the little things and never give up. Keep putting one foot in front of the other. That is the only way to get to where you want to go.

Go after your dreams. You are worthy and you can do it. Anything is possible. I believe in you. Now it is time for you to start believing in yourself.

ABOUT THE AUTHOR
TARRYN REEVES

Tarryn Reeves is a conscious disruptor heading up her two impactful businesses. She is the head marketing witch of Zimpasha (her creative marketing agency and epic team of VAs) and is the book bitch of Four Eagles Publishing (her publishing company for conscious disruptors and thought leaders who want to make an impact with their writing).

She is a *USA Today* best-selling author, book coach, publisher and visibility expert whose work has been featured in the *Los Angeles Times*, World News Network, Thrive Global and more.

Together with her team she works with high-level entrepreneurs to get loud and visible to create ripple effects of impact with their message across the globe.

She resides in Australia with her husband, daughter and a myriad of animals. When she isn't creating best-sellers and coming up with remarkable marketing strategies, she can be found nurturing her garden or reading a good book.

Connect with Tarryn here: *www.tarrynreeves.com*

Facebook: *www.facebook.com/tarrynreevesthepublishingexpert*
Instagram: *www.instagram.com/tarryn.reeves*
LinkedIn: *www.linkedin.com/in/tarrynreeves*
Youtube: *www.youtube.com/channel/UC59D0dqA62qDeULziX1VOGQ*
Facebook: *www.facebook.com/tarrynreevesthepublishingexpert*

YVETTE MAYER

FROM STUCK AND DRAINED TO
LIT UP AND LIBERATED

When she told me I wasn't going back to school after the holidays, and she'd enrolled me in secretarial college, I couldn't believe my good fortune!

Holy moly, not only was I freeeeee, but maybe I could get a job and marry my sexy older boyfriend? I remember it clearly, 15-year-old me was absolutely thrilled.

Here's why.

Mum and I went to the same selective high school (Fort Street High School), where academia ruled ... and university was encouraged. I inherited Mum's high IQ, preference for sport over schoolwork and need for approval. Struggling to keep up with my highly motivated peers, like my mum before me, my grades fell as my teenage hormones raged.

But I'm getting ahead of myself now.

I thrived in secretarial college. Shorthand was fun, treating typing as a race appealed to my competitive side and effortlessly sitting at the top of the class was great for my ego.

Then came my first 'grown-up' J.O.B. as receptionist at a local business. I could even walk there. Result!

But a girl changes a LOT between 15 and 17.

As it turned out, while 15-year-old me was content with being a high school dropout receptionist … 17-year-old me had other ideas.

Note to all, do NOT listen to 15-year-olds. They're dominated by hormones and instant gratification. At least I was. They're not to be trusted, so be patient with them. When you're not being patient, be forceful. I mean to say, make them stay in school!

At 17, I was ready for more. Having spent a work experience week at a leading ad agency in Year 10 (thanks to a high-flying family friend), my mind was made up. I was ready to get my foot in the door and, as it would happen, on the ladder.

I didn't really know much about the advertising world, mind you. Just that the people seemed to have a LOT of fun at work and do interesting things (like make TV commercials). Also said family friends were considered rich. No brainer, I wanted in, and my only goal was to land an admin job, NOT a secretarial one. From there, I was convinced I could work my way up.

The year was 1989, and the ad industry was in its heyday when I sauntered into my 'dream job': thumbing through every (single) newspaper in the country, collecting 'tear sheets' for proof ad appearance, on behalf of the Federal Government. I'm talking regional and suburban press too, 100s of papers every day. My hands were perpetually black but I was happy as a pig in newspaper print!

The little girl who struggled in high school was long gone. In her place a dedicated, committed, ambitious girl-woman. I loved everything about it (outside of not being old enough to drink at the agency bar)!

Over the next nine years I went on to quadruple my salary and land a lead role on Australia's largest airline. I drove a convertible 4WD, spent an inordinate amount on designer fashion and my weekends on dancefloors.

'I've made it!'

But what exactly had I made?

The expectations on me were higher than ever before. I distinctly recall the words 'early mark Mayer' being thrown my way, if I dared leave before 8pm – 11pm finishes were encouraged.

I repeated mantras like 'work hard, play hard' or 'you're a long time dead' ... barely sleeping on the weekends, while working 60–80 hours a week.

Something had to give. And that something was ME.

I was running up heartbreak hill during the Sydney City2Surf when I had my first panic attack ... OMG I thought, *I've started having panic attacks.* This is how they get you. The fear of having another creating the vicious cycle.

My bosses were less than thrilled when I took medical leave. But I was so riddled with anxiety, the thought of leading a client meeting floored me.

This was defining moment number one.

I felt nauseous returning to my job as I could see how toxic the environment was. And I came to realize the relationship I was in could be described with the T word too.

So I decided to run: away from the 10-year-long career, the boyfriend and even the country.

And my mind was made up.

Advertising wasn't for me. It was too shallow. Much too stressful. So I would re-imagine my career, after doing the European backpacker thing.

But it didn't quite unfold that way ...

217

I ran out of cash a few months later, discovered I was a hopeless secretary (much harder than I remembered), and found myself at the door of the London office of the agency I'd recently departed.

Gratefully, they welcomed me in and a funny thing happened. It turned out I didn't hate the industry ... just the bully of a boss I'd left behind.

Two years later back on home soil I was much more discerning in my choice of role. Hotly in demand, I took the 'lesser' role with my gut leading the way. I would go on to stay with the business for 17 years, spanning two continents.

It wasn't without incident though.

With my anxiety under control, my career catapulted forward. By my late thirties I even had a 'C' in my title – Chief Digital Officer of Australia. Yep, that self-initiated lateral move to run the digital team proved very wise!

My love life on the other hand ... not so thriving! I even wrote a blog for a bit there: 'The husband hunt'. Did. Not. Find. A. Husband.

At 39, I'd just met my latest in a string of intense but short relationships when my world turned upside down.

Cut to defining moment number two.

'You have breast cancer.'

What?! Things like that don't happen to me!!!

Until they do ...

It was the whole shebang: double mastectomy, chemotherapy and a full year of hospital-based treatments.

So what did I do? I worked through it.

You read that right.

My career defined me. The business needed me. Also, it took my mind off my mortality.

And yet … I knew the gig was up.

I couldn't muster the enthusiasm for the things I'd once considered important.

The type of work I did, again felt shallow.

I thought to myself, if I were to die soon, would I be proud of the impact I'd made in the world?

NOPE.

A deep knowing took hold … that I had so much untapped potential and a desire to make a positive contribution in the world.

But how? All I'd ever known was my advertising career. It was a career that had given me so much, including a luxury lifestyle, a home in a popular inner-city suburb, a share in a holiday home and a convertible Audi.

I pondered this and didn't have an answer.

But the Universe did.

A friend who'd been living in New York returned home to undergo chemo, while I was still in treatment. While we weren't incredibly close, she'd called me with her shitty news and I encouraged her to come home for treatment: 'You NEED your family around you.'

It turned out that her initial treatments were shorter than mine and we were to finish up around the same time. As our friendship grew closer we hatched a plan.

Me: 'I just don't know what to do with myself, I CAN NOT stay here, in the same job, house etc., after all this.' Nicole: 'Get a transfer to NYC. We can live together and you can figure out the rest of your life from there.'

Winding back the clock a little: just three months before my diagnosis I'd spent part of my long service leave doing a house swap (I swapped my house for a shoe box in Murray Hill). And I'd had the thought, *Gosh I love NY, I think I could live here.*

Within eight weeks of my treatment finishing … I actually did.

I'm forever grateful for the experience and to the business that made it possible, shipping me and my chemo pressie (Chilli Sparkles the cavoodle) across the world.

It was the BEST possible way for me to reconnect with my joy.

I'm a wanderluster.

It lights me up. The newness! My eyes were continually wide as I showed up to my office on Broadway and travelled across the country (and the world) all expenses paid.

In our NYC apartment, however, things were heavy. Nic's cancer had spread.

We couldn't believe it. I still can't.

For that first year in NY, I balanced work with being Nic's number one support team as she tried drug after drug, which meant both holding space for her to grieve AND making sure the moments counted.

We travelled a lot: Jamaica, Bali, the Hamptons, New Orleans, the Catskills and the slopes of Park City and Aspen, darlings!

Nicole showed me what it looks like to navigate running out of hope … with grace. Chilli became a support dog too (which was a beautiful thing). After a year, the decision for her to move home was inevitable.

From the other side of the world I hung on to the words in her blog 'a year of gratitude'.

Less than a year later I found myself on a plane to Australia to say goodbye. Soon after that, she was gone.

Grieving Nic, her words of wisdom reverberated …

'experiences are more important than things'
'there's a space between stimulus and response … use it'
'life is not about the number of days but the number of moments'

Back in NYC, I decided, YES Chilli can sleep in my bed after all!

And I went back to work … although it took me a while to BE back at work.

That said, my role in the US was incredible. I was continually asked with a stressed-out inflection, 'So what's it like in NY compared to Sydney?'

#truthbomb … far better resourced, more days off and a level of independence I'd never experienced before.

With my head office in Chicago and clients in the likes of LA and Nashville, I travelled extensively and used every single one of our 'available days of leave' … unlike my far too busy peers … No way José, gimme all the experiences!

The Cannes Advertising festival? ... Yes please. A work trip to London? ... Jolly good! South by Southwest (in Austin, Texas) ... Cheers to that! How about Disneyland for Comicon? ... Pick me!

My appetite for summer in the Hamptons was legendary too, with summer Fridays regularly turning into whole (instead of half) days.

Meantime I did GOOD at work and even got myself promoted to Executive Vice President.

But it wasn't all beer and skittles.

In 2015 I showed my physio a lump in my thigh, which I thought had something to do with all the running I was doing leading up to the NYC marathon: 'That's not muscular, you should see a doctor, given your history.'

When the doctor called with my results she asked if I had company ... It was a Friday night and Chilli and I were home alone. 'JUST TELL ME!'

'It's either a new cancer (sarcoma) or a secondary spread from your breast cancer and it's 11cm in circumference.'

Google told me I was dying.

Defining moment numero tres!

I called home and my sister got on the next flight.

We spent a week alternating between oncology appointments and exploring NYC together.

Only to discover said lump was a rare tumour (a desmoid) and NOT malignant!

The upside – a renewed determination to figure out my next career move. Once again I had considered my legacy and come up short.

My longing for improved health led me in the direction of Health Coaching Training. I followed that up with Yoga Teacher training

But I just couldn't work out how I could continue my luxe life in either direction … and I was naturally terrified.

When I next visited Sydney on holiday, fate stepped in again.

Which brings me to my head-hunting finale!

Defining moment number four.

My grown-up dream job (from another life) was presented to me.

Managing Director of the Sydney office of the one agency I'd long admired. The largest single office of its kind in the country, 300 staff, hundreds of millions in billings.

I said NO.

I even explained my predicament … I wanted out of the industry. But the wooing was relentless: 'You've worked for the same group for 17 years. This will be different.'

With my parents' health declining, the call to be shipped home (all expenses paid) in a 'cherry on top' kind of role, made too much sense.

So instead of leaving the industry as planned, I found myself in the highest pressured role of my career.

I had pure intentions. I decided this would be my last hoorah and I would go out as a legend of the industry.

Here's what happened instead …

A return to a smaller market, with tiny margins, where the staff are spread too thin.

Bullying style clients that demanded meetings starting at 7pm.

Working through the night to be told, it's not up to scratch...

Nailing my KPIs, while feeling like a failure.

Nights lying awake, stomach churning and heart racing.

My anxiety returned with a vengeance.

On reflection, it was a good thing.

It wasn't that I couldn't handle the role, but that I didn't want to.

My soul was no longer whispering, it was screaming.

And that's the story of how I became a corporate dropout.

Defining moment number five!

Eighteen months later, I gave my notice.

I'd started a side hustle in network marketing and I had high hopes that it would help me realize my potential.

For the next six months I worked four days a week and spent the other one (and weekends) on my business. It grew.

When I left the corporate world in December 2018, I felt both relief and fear.

I was finally FREEEEEEE ... but also, how do I pay my huge wad of bills?

As I was lying on my kinesiologist's table around this time she asked me, 'How do you want to feel?' The words 'lit up and liberated' flew out of my mouth. I got goosies …

Hello again Universe!

The Lit Up & Liberated Movement was a download from a higher source, meant for me. It's since become my North Star and mission.

Soon after, I realized my mission was bigger than the oils I was selling … also cash flow said pivot!

So I assessed my situation:

- Skills: business, marketing/sales, mentoring, leadership
- Passion: wellbeing
- Network: largely corporate

So in April 2019, a campaign began on LinkedIn to grow Yvette Mayer Wellbeing, a coaching and wellbeing consultancy, designed to support the businesses I'd grown up in to take better care of their people.

I hired my first Business Coach (Wow! That's a thing?!) who helped me market my personal brand.

The consultancy work was slow going … on the other hand, coaching enquiries began to flood in.

All those years in corporate had earned me an amazing reputation and that opened the door to coaching demand.

That's how I found myself coaching incredible humans on everything from business to health, life and leadership.

My heart exploded.

I was finally getting paid to make a positive impact on other human's lives. Not only that, but they reflected back the ripple effects of my support. Happier teams, partners and children!

The consulting took a back seat as my coaching load grew.

But I quickly realized 1:1 was only the first step. I needed a bigger platform, and a more scalable impact.

I determined that the next step was in group coaching ... and with that, three months into my coaching career, I launched the inaugural 'Lit Up and Liberated' program.

It brought in $100k overnight.

Jokes.

It flopped. As in zero sign-ups.

To be fair, outside of seeing other coaches do this sort of thing successfully, I didn't really know what I was doing.

Things I didn't have:

- A niche
- A mailing list
- A big following
- An understanding of how to create demand in the lead-up to the launch (or even any lead-up ha-ha)

The flop knocked my confidence briefly but more importantly it solidified my desire for this kind of impact.

The process unlocked an appetite to truly become a digital CEO of a seven-figure business and I knew it to be my destiny. This WAS the road to fulfilling my potential.

It was time to back myself and go for it.

I invested what savings I had left into two things:

- A 3-month course creation program
- A 12-month high level digital CEO Mastermind

Not going to lie, my ego struggled through the early days. I mean here I was, the outgoing boss of a 300-person office, a veritable BIG WIG, and I felt so small.

My next course was a *tiny* success.

My 1:1 coaching rates doubled, then tripled.

But the biggest shift came when, in May 2020, I claimed my space as a Business Coach.

As it turned out, running away from corporate toward health was a steppingstone.

My business exploded the day I connected the dots between my corporate background and passion for helping women feel lit up and liberated by building a business on their own terms.

Eighteen months later my business has grown to multiple six figures and I've helped 100s of women cash in on their years of experience and wisdom to step into digital CEO mode. Often this means supporting them to integrate digital products into their business model, because that's exactly how I exploded my impact (and upped my freedom!).

I run Masterminds, have a digital product focused course and work with clients 1:1.

And I'm so thrilled to witness the ripple effect of my efforts:

Take Tricia Camacho (based in North Carolina) who I've guided from 'my course isn't selling' to increasingly bigger launches and a membership with 65+ pattern making enthusiasts. 'Seriously Yvette, I couldn't do this without you, you are the best business coach ever.'

Elisia Florio, who came to me with a longing for a business and little direction … to now being CEO of naturalmum.com.au. 'Yvette, I can do this without you but I don't want to.'

And Brianna Graydon from Pink Cow Social whose signature course sold out on the first launch. 'I feel like a proper business owner, contributing to my family because of you.'

Told you this is it.

Defining moment number six.

I once dreamed of living as a nomad, the old 'laptop lifestyle' featuring on my vision boards from as far back as my 20s.

Little did I know that, aged 50, I would be living it.

As I type this chapter, I come to you from an Airbnb in beautiful Byron Bay – we've been on the road for nine months.

Chilli Sparkles is curled up in a ball on the couch.

I'm typing on my laptop with a big fat smile on my face and we're about to head to the beach.

This is life + business created on purpose.

The path to realizing more of my potential.

And it's got me feeling all the Lit Up & Liberated™ feels.

ABOUT THE AUTHOR
YVETTE MAYER

Yvette Mayer is a global business and marketing coach, with a 30-year background in corporate marketing.

She walked out of her career determined to feel more lit up and liberated and makes it her mission to help others do the same.

Yvette helps women cash in on their years of experience and wisdom, by growing an online business and claiming their role as CEO. She supports her clients to unlock purposeful, profitable, scalable growth with digital products (e.g. webinars, courses, memberships, group programs).

She is a highly regarded leader, speaker, coach, mentor and mindset 'magician'. She balances her business with exploring the world digital nomad style, with her doggy Chilli Sparkles.

You can connect with Yvette at *www.yvettemayer.com*

Facebook Page: *www.facebook.com/yvettemayercoaching*
Instagram: *www.instagram.com/yvettemayer_*
LinkedIn: *www.linkedin.com/in/yvettemmayer*

ABOUT THE PUBLISHER
FOUR EAGLES PUBLISHING

Four Eagles Publishing is the publishing house of choice for innovators, rule-breakers, visionaries, disruptors and leaders.

Four Eagles truly appreciates their storytelling because we share the same foundation of authenticity.

Tying creativity and business together is an art. Handling the positioning of your business, increasing your social media presence, expanding your audience, and attracting new opportunities works hand in hand with your message and inner gifts and we know how to present this to the world.

We have one goal: to create a joyful and simple process for writing, publishing and marketing your best-selling book.

Publishing a book is as simple as being you.

If you are ready to write, publish and market your book then get in touch with us today: *www.foureaglespublishing.com*

Facebook: www.facebook.com/Four-Eagles-Publishing-102701058950915
Instagram: www.instagram.com/foureaglespublishing
LinkedIn: www.linkedin.com/company/77730413/admin
Pinterest: www.pinterest.com.au/tarrynreevespublisher/_created
YouTube:
www.youtube.com/channel/UCXW3EmqAAkpUEMYc_0mqGWQ
Facebook Group:
www.facebook.com/groups/theauthorsloungefoureaglespublishing
Podcast: www.theauthorsloungepodcast.com.au

Made in United States
North Haven, CT
12 April 2022

18177664R10148